FOUNDATIONS OF EXTERNAL QUALITY ASSURANCE IN INDIAN HIGHER EDUCATION

About NAAC

The National Assessment and Accreditation Council (NAAC) is an autonomous organization, established by the University Grants Commission (UGC) in 1994, with its headquarters at Bangalore. The main function of NAAC is to assess and accredit institutions of higher education. The process of assessment and accreditation involves preparation of a Self-Study Report of the institution and validation of the same by the on-site visit of a team of assessors. The outcome of assessment and accreditation will be a grade which is valid up to 5 years. As of January 2003, more than three hundred institutions of higher education have been assessed by NAAC and there is an overall appreciation for the intrinsic benefits of quality assessment in the country.

Website: www.naac-india.com

About the Authors

Antony Stella is the Adviser of the National Assessment and Accreditation Council (NAAC). As one of the first staff of NAAC, she has been a part of all the developmental activities of NAAC for the past six years. With a Ph.D. in Educational Technology, she has published in both educational technology and quality assurance. She has more than 75 papers and seven books – three on Assessment and Accreditation and the rest on Education – to her credit. She has authored a Report for UNESCO about external quality assurance in India. She is the Project Director of the Impact Analysis of Accreditation funded by the Ministry for Human Resource Development. She is the recipient of Shastri Indo-Canadian Faculty Research Award and Fulbright Post-doctoral Fellowship.

A. Gnanam is a leading Plant Molecular Biologist turned academic administrator. After his earlier education in India, he went to US on a Fulbright fellowship for the Ph.D degree from N. Carolina State University, Raleigh, N.C. He taught for a couple of years at Cornel University, Ithaca, N.Y., before returning to India in 1968. At Madurai Kamaraj University, Madurai where he pursued his academic and science career, he had established the now well known School of Biological Sciences and one of three National Centres for Plant Molecular Biology. He is a Fellow and Senior Vice President of Indian National Science Academy, New Delhi and the Academy of Sciences, Allahabad.

Prof. Gnanam has been the Vice-Chancellor of three universities for almost 14 years. Currently, he is Chairman of the Executive and other statutory bodies of National Assessment and Accreditation Council (NAAC) and a member of the Board of the International Network of Quality Assurance Agencies for Higher Education (INQAAHE). He is also a member of the Global Forum on Higher Education constituted by the UNESCO.

FOUNDATIONS OF EXTERNAL QUALITY ASSURANCE IN INDIAN HIGHER EDUCATION

ANTONY STELLA

A. GNANAM

CONCEPT PUBLISHING COMPANY, NEW DELHI-110059

ISBN 81-8069-048-2

First Published 2001
Second Revised Edition 2003

Published and Printed by
Ashok Kumar Mittal
Concept Publishing Company
A/15-16, Commercial Block, Mohan Garden
New Delhi-110059 (INDIA)

Phones : 25351460, 25351794
Fax : 091-11-25357103
E-mail : publishing@conceptpub.com

Foreword

Prof. A Gnanam and Dr. Antony Stella have done a great service to the cause of higher education in India by writing this erudite and scintillating book on accreditation and assurance. Being the top managers of the NAAC, they are the best fitted to provide an inside view of the policy parameters as well as the nitty-gritty issues. I compliment them on having achieved the formidable task of writing an eminently readable book on the otherwise dry subject.

It is somewhat surprising to a layman like me that the interest in accreditation and assurance is not very strong in academic circles in India. There is a certain apathy, if not antipathy, to the concept. I have heard some teachers refer pejoratively to the 5-star culture which NAAC promotes. There is also a pervasive feeling of the apprehension that there will be sweeping, subjective judgments about a whole institution, department or course and that there cannot be any foolproof system of objective assessment of quality.

No doubt, quality is an elusive virtue and it is not easy to measure it in mathematically exact terms. But what the entire exercise promotes is introspection and self-assessment, peer-group validation, a kind of opinion gathering from the various stakeholders and a transparent public rating by a nationally respected independent body. There can be misjudgments in terms of fine-tuning of ratings, but it would be a rare occurrence for a national body to give a rating wide off the mark. In any case, the outcry that an undeserved assessment would generate is itself the best safeguard against unwitting or deliberate errors of judgment.

I commend this book to all those seriously interested in upgrading the quality of higher education in India.

New Delhi
25th November, 2000

Maharaj Krishen Kaw
Secretary
(Secondary and Higher Education)
Government of India

Preface

Assessment and Accreditation as an External Quality Assurance (EQA) mechanism for higher education has emerged as the most widely accepted and adopted methodology throughout the world during the past decade. It is the considered option, evolving out of the plethora of traditional mechanisms such as inspection, control, affiliation and recognition. These regulatory methods, which are by and large in-built checks and balances to oversee the system, are internal, non-comparable with other institutions and fragmentary in nature. When the system of education was relatively small, catering to a few, and when it was supported mostly by the public funds, they were possibly sufficient. But the situation has changed rapidly in the last two decades in an unprecedented manner. With the world becoming a global village, imparting higher education of nationally comparable and internationally acceptable 'standards' to a larger population of students has become essential and urgent. This perception has resulted in the worldwide acceptance of External Quality Assurance to ensure the quality of education and to make the system more responsive to the demand for accountability. In India, very much in line with this international trend, without the usual time lag, the national agency for assessment and accreditation – National Assessment and Accreditation Council (NAAC) was established in 1994 on the recommendations of the National Policy of Education as prioritised in the Programme of Action (PoA) document.

Meanwhile, External Quality Assurance (EQA) and its instruments like Academic Audit, Assessment and Accreditation have grown into a science and art. There are far more articles and books published on this than the entire higher education system in the recent years. The articles are mostly based on the interest and experience of more than hundred national agencies functioning in all the countries committed to Quality Assurance. However, the quality movement itself being less than a decade old, the literature available on EQA and its processes is scarce in India.

NAAC has been active in its formative years in absorbing, evolving and adopting the EQA mechanisms and in operationalizing them in the Indian context. We published a series of articles as a part of our mission to propagate the concept to gain the acceptability. When we decided to compile those articles, 'Books Plus' gave a nice shape to it as a book and the first edition was released in 2001. It covered the developments till 2000. With spectacular developments during the next two years, we realized the need to bring out the next edition with appropriate updates and the Concept Publishing Company has done a wonderful job for this second edition. We hope that this updated compendium will be a useful source of reference to those interested in quality assurance efforts in the Indian context.

1st January, 2003
Bangalore

Dr. Antony Stella
and
Prof. A. Gnanam

Acknowledgements

We are grateful to AIU, NIEPA and *The Hindu* for their consent to reproduce the articles authored by us and published by them earlier.

We are happy to acknowledge the generous support given to the first author by the Shastri Indo-Canadian Institute, New Delhi through the faculty research award, which facilitated library research and interaction with the quality assurance system of Canada, and helped in enriching the comparative perspective of this book.

Dr. Antony Stella
and
Prof. A. Gnanam

Contents

Appendices

Abbreviations

AB	Accreditation Board
ABET	Accreditation Board for Engineering and Technology
AECD	Advanced Education and Career Development
AIACHE	All India Association of Christian Higher Education
AICTE	All India Council for Technical Education
AIU	Association of Indian Universities
BITS	Birla Institute of Technology and Science
CBCS	Choice Based Credit System
CEEC	Commission for Evaluation of College Education
CINDA	Centro Interuniversitario De Desarrollo
DCE	Directorate of Collegiate Education
DCI	Dental Council of India
DEC	Distance Education Council
DETYA	Department of Education, Training and Youth Affairs
DST	Department of Science and Technology
EAIE	European Association for International Education
EC	Executive Committee
ECTS	European Credit Transfer System
ENIC	European Network of Information Centers on Recognition and Mobility
EQA	External Quality Assurance
GATE	Global Alliance for Transnational Education
GATS	General Agreement on Trade in Services
GC	General Council
GNP	Gross National Product
GoI	Government of India
HEFCE	Higher Education Funding Council of England
HEI	Higher Education Institution
HEQC	Higher Education Quality Council
HRI	Highly Rated Institutions
IAU	International Association of Universities
ICAR	Indian Council of Agricultural Research
IIM	Indian Institute of Management
IIQ	International Institute for Quality
IIT	Indian Institute of Technology

INC	Indian Nursing Council
INQAAHE	International Network of Quality Assurance Agencies in Higher Education
IQAC	Internal Quality Assurance Cell
IQRP	Internationalisation of Quality Review Project
ISO	International Organisation for Standardisation
MCI	Medical Council of India
MHRD	Ministry of Human Resource Development
MoA	Memorandum of Association
MoU	Memorandum of Understanding
NAAC	National Assessment and Accreditation Council
NABHE	National Accreditation Board for Higher Education
NAFSA	National Association of Foreign Students Advisers
NARIC	Network of National Academic Recognition Information Center
NBA	National Board of Accreditation
NCTE	National Council for Teacher Education
NIIT	National Institute of Information Technology
NPE	National Policy on Education
NSS	National Social Service
OCGS	Ontario Council for Graduate Studies
OCUA	Ontario Council of University Affairs
OECD	Organisation for Economic Co-operation and Development
PHE	Private Higher Education
PI	Performance Indicator
PoA	Programme of Action
QAA	Quality Assurance Agency
QAI	Quality Assurance International
QCI	Quality Council of India
R&D	Research and Development
RAE	Research Assessment Exercise
S&T	Science and Technology
TEXT	Trans European Exchange and Transfer Consortium
TRACE	Trans Regional Academic Mobility and Credential Evaluation
UCJ	University Council of Jamaica
UGC	University Grants Commission
UHE	Universalisation of Higher Education
UNESCO	United Nations Educational, Scientific and Cultural Organisation
WTO	World Trade Organisation

Part I: Emergence of EQA

The shift to formal system of External Quality Assurance (EQA) evident across many countries and regions is the most significant trend seen in the higher education provisions over the last decade or so. Academic audit, assessment and accreditation as the major instruments of EQA, are consequently emerging as an art and science. In India, very much in line with this international trend, without the usual time lag, the national agency for assessment and accreditation – National Assessment and Accreditation Council (NAAC) was established in 1994 on the recommendations of the National Policy of Education as prioritised in the Programme of Action (PoA) document. This part presents the background against which the National External Quality Assurance mechanism by NAAC emerged and evolved in India. It also explains the relevance of NAAC in the Indian context.

1 Emerging Trends in Higher Education

Education, particularly higher education as the instrument of individual, societal and economic transformation is well recognised now more than ever. Consequently, there have been greater interest and investment in higher education the world over with the concomitant increase in the number of students who opt for higher education. This demand for higher education from a sizeable portion of the population is going to continue during the years to come. In addition to the need for the expansion of higher education, there are a number of political and socio-economic factors that affect the development of the system of higher education in any country. In order to cope with these challenges effectively and efficiently, it is essential that the educational institutions have a realistic understanding of the emerging trends and the role they have to play to build a better future. This chapter is about these emerging trends and their implications for the higher education institutions.

The higher education system is witnessing significant transformations and reforms, including the emergence of new types of institutions and the higher education landscape is changing very fast. Today, there are universities without building or classrooms or even a library. There are universities located thousands of miles away from its students in a different continent. There are higher education institutions (HEIs) open 24 hours a day, seven days a week, 365 days a year. There are HEIs that offer degrees with a catalogue of hundreds of courses. These developments that seem to be imaginative are indeed realities. Soon the system may introduce degrees valid only for five years after graduation and colleges willing to reimburse its students if they do not find a suitable job within six months after graduation. With the developments in WTO and GATS we will soon have countries whose main export earnings come from the sale of higher education services. (Salmi, J., 2000) There are also changes in patterns of financing and governance, establishment of external quality assurance mechanisms, reforms in curriculum design, and technological innovations for teaching-learning. In this rapidly changing scenario, the higher education institutions are expected to quickly adapt to emerging developments and plan for a better future. The prerequisite to plan for a better future is an understanding of the changes and their impact on the system of higher education.

An analysis of the changing context reveals the following trends, most of which are likely to permeate through the educational policies and practices of the next few decades:

Trend I

1.1 Shift from elitist to mass education
1.2 Continuing quantitative expansion

Trend II

2.1 Decreasing funding from governmental sources
2.2 Debate on higher education as a non-merit item
2.3 Increasing demand for non-formal and life-long learning

2.4 Socio-political pressure based on demographic, political, and socio-economic changes
2.5 Increasing private initiatives
2.6 Increasing influence of market forces

Trend III

3.1 Focus on science and technology
3.2 Shift from mono- to multi- and inter-disciplinarity
3.3 Rethinking the role of universities

Trend IV

4.1 Quality Assurance

Trend I

Trend I is the much-discussed scenario of higher education, which is based on the explicitly observable changes in the system. Two of these changes — shift towards mass education and quantitative expansion — need a mention here. For a long time India did not have any organised way of educating the people. The *Gurukula* system was prevalent in the country, which made access to education very difficult for a common man. The shift from the *Gurukula* system to an organised system of education in the middle of 19th century is a British legacy. That was followed by the quantitative expansion gradually in the early part of the 20th century.

1.1 Shift from Elitist to Mass Education

The faith and consequently the focused attention on higher education as an instrument for the socio-economic transformation of a nation became even more intense the world over in the post Second World War period. The Second World War made the countries realise the benefits of skill and knowledge and hence the need for human resource that was capable of more than being merely a literate. Higher education was seen as the instrument that could develop the necessary skill and knowledge among the human resource and that led to the quantitative expansion in terms of the number of higher education institutions and consequently in student enrolment the world over. Similar trend could be witnessed in India as well. At the time of independence, in 1947, there were only 21 universities and 500 colleges in the country. A cursory look at the following table indicates the quantitative expansion that took place during the post-independent era.

Table 1: Growth in Institutions of Higher Education

Year	*Number of Universities*	*Number of Colleges*	*Student Enrolment (in millions)*
1947	21	500	0.20
1950-51	30	750	0.26
1960-61	49	1537	0.65
1970-71	93	3604	1.95
1980-81	123	4722	2.75
1990-91	177	7346	4.43
2000-01	259	10750	7.40
2002	274	12600	8.00

(www.education.nic.in, Universities Handbook, 28th edition)

1.2 Continuing Quantitative Expansion

The increase in student enrolment seems to be impressive in India but it is not different from the experience of other nations. Worldwide, there has been a near seven-fold expansion in the number of students from 13 million in 1960 to 82 million in 1985 (UNESCO, 1998), and 85 million at the turn of the century. In absolute terms India has succeeded to a great extent in providing increased access as the number of students in higher education has registered a phenomenal 40-fold increase from about 0.20 million in 1947 to about 8 million in 2002. However, its impact becomes nullified due to the growing population here, as compared to other countries.

A World Bank-UNESCO Task Force on Higher Education

and Society in its report (World Bank, 2000; Bloom and Rosovsky, 2001) has drawn attention to the fact that while India's tertiary enrolment rate of 613 per 100,000 population compares favourably with that of many sub-Saharan African countries it is well below the averages of other developing regions such as Latin America (1638) and the Middle East and North Africa (1465) and extremely low in comparison with Europe and Central Asia (2436) and the United States (5339). The implication of the quantitative expansion, though is well below the desirable level, has resulted in many fold increase in expenditure on higher education.

Table 2: Expenditure on Higher Education (1951-52 to 1993-94)

Year	*Expenditure (in '000 Rs.)*	*Per Student Expenditure in Rs.*
1951-52	72,319	416
1961-62	3,44,931	639
1971-72	8,35,982	428
1981-82	9,55,309	1800
1991-92	2,44,27,774	5522
1993-94	2,91,55,611	4537

Expenditure on higher education has registered a considerable increase from Rs. 7.23 crores in 1951-52 to Rs. 2915.56 crores in 1993. Despite the increase by 11 times in per student expenditure the students have not benefited much due to inflation. In terms of the relative proportion to the national income, the percentage has increased from 0.2 to 0.5 during this period. In spite of such steep increase in student enrolment, number of institutions and consequent expenditure on higher education, the Indian higher education system still caters only to 6 per cent of the relevant age group of 17 to 23 years. This is abysmally low in comparison to the over 50 per cent obtained in the OECD countries, and 20 per cent considered essential for sustained economic development. (Powar, 2000a) Even the South East Asian neighbours of India show much higher enrolment such as in the Philippines (27.8 per cent), Thailand (19.0 per cent) and Malaysia (10.1 per cent). (Joshi, M.M., 1998)

Even though the same trend, in terms of quantitative expansion, expenditure, and shift towards mass education, has been witnessed in the other countries, the developed countries like UK, USA and Germany have succeeded in providing higher education to nearly 50 per cent of the relevant age group. Consequently these countries have shown tremendous growth and development in terms of national prosperity. This indicates lack of preparedness of the country to meet the challenges of this trend.

While Trend I could be observed explicitly as simple phenomena, Trend II is, to a large extent, set by the impact of the various societal, political, governmental and economic changes of the country — the forces that are complex, interrelated and multi-dimensional.

Trend II

2.1 Decreasing Funding from Government Sources

Many of the problems involving higher education are rooted in a lack of resources. For example, developing countries spend far less than developed countries on each student. Although absolute spending per student is low, developing countries already face a huge expenditure on higher education, with a smaller income than the developed world and with public spending for education growing more quickly than the income. (World Bank, 2000)

India has the second largest system of higher education and is one of the lowest per capita income countries in the world. In the context of the on going economic reforms, a major problem which decision makers confront today is how to provide financial sustenance for the system. The changing perception on the subsidisation of higher education by the government further accentuates this problem. Government has been the major source of funding higher education. Since independence, the government contribution to higher education in absolute quantity has been increasing while the funding from the other sources has been on the decline. Table 3 gives the details of this trend.

Data also reveals that the share of higher education sector in the total outlay for education in the five-year plans remained between 11 per cent and 13 per cent during 1951-52 to 1991-92. It was only in 1981-82, that higher education could receive 15 per cent. Even this percentage is much lower than that of many developed countries. The expenditure on higher education, as percentage of GNP has fallen from 0.98 per cent in 1980-81 to 0.35 per cent in 1994-95. (Powar, 2002) Table 4 gives the details of the declining share of higher education out of the total educational budget.

Table 3: Sources of income of educational institutions

(*in percent*)

Year	*Govt. funds (Centre & State)*	*Local Bodies funds*	*University funds*	*Fees*	*Endowments*
1950-51	57.06	10.93	—	20.39	11.62
1960-61	67.97	6.53	—	17.14	8.35
1970-71	75.65	4.34	1.36	12.81	5.85
1980-81	81.70	4.71	1.37	8.20	4.03

Source: Ministry of HRD, India.

In the First Five Year Plan, allocation to higher education was only 9 per cent. The allocations were almost doubled in the Second Five Year Plan and declined slightly in the Third Five Year Plan. The allocations in the Fourth, Fifth and Sixth Plans were relatively high, but declined slightly in the subsequent Five Year Plans and reached 8 per cent in the Eighth Five Year Plan. This is the lowest so far, less than the allocation made in the First Five Year Plan.

Even adult education gets higher allocation than the entire higher education in the last plan. The allocation to adult education in the sixth and the eighth plans was 9 per cent. If the responsibility of adult education is given to the elementary and secondary education sectors, the flow of funds to school education will not only strengthen the infrastructure facilities and support services of the school but also lead to optimum utilisation of available resources including human resource.

Table 4: Plan Expenditure on Different Sectors of Education (in per cent)

Sector	*I Plan 1951-56*	*II Plan 1956-61*	*III Plan 1961-66*	*Plan Holiday 1966-69*	*IV Plan 1969-74*	*V Plan 1974-79*	*VI Plan 1980-85*	*VII Plan 1985-90*	*Plan Holiday*	*VIII Plan 1992-97*
Elementary Education	56	35	34	24	30	35	33	37	37	47
Secondary Education	13	19	18	16	18	17	21	24	22	18
Adult Education	—	—	—	—	—	—	9	6	9	9
Higher Education	9	18	15	24	25	22	22	16	12	8
Technical Education	13	18	21	25	13	12	11	14	17	14
Others	9	10	12	11	14	14	4	3	2	4
Total	100	100	100	100	100	100	100	100	100	100

Source: Govt. of India (1995), Budgetary resources for education (1951-52-1993-94): MHRD.

Comparison between the allocations for adult education and higher education during these plan periods reveals that the priority given to adult education is consistent while the funding pattern of higher education is towards steady decline from 22 per cent in 1980-85 to 8 per cent in 1992-97. In fact, in the eighth plan, school and adult education put together get 74 per cent while higher education gets a meagre 9 per cent. This trend of increasing priority to adult education and declining support to higher education needs a critical analysis.

In sum, higher education in India is in deep financial strain, with escalating costs and increasing needs, on the one hand, and shrinking budgetary resources, on the other. The share of higher education in total planned resources was 1.24 in the fourth five-year plan. But ever since, it has declined continuously to 0.53 per cent in the seventh five-year plan and further down to 0.35 per cent in the eighth five-year plan (1992-97), though the actual expenditure has increased by more than 100 times from Rs. 140 million in the first five-year plan to Rs. 15,000 million in the eighth five-year plan at current prices, and 6.5 times in terms of real prices. Thus although higher education in India is characterised by massive public investment, this investment is still regarded as much below the optimum. (Joshi, M.M., 1998)

2.2 Debate on Higher Education as Non-merit Item

The world over, education, particularly higher education is considered to be a national investment except perhaps in the United States of America, where it is treated as a means of enhancing the personal benefits of the individual. Yet, the country subsidises higher education up to 50 per cent of the budget even in the so-called private universities through student aid fund and special schemes. Germany, France, Great Britain and all other developed countries treat higher education as a national investment and, therefore, make it mandatory for the state to provide easy access to all citizens with adequate support for tuition fee. There may be differential tuition fee structure for foreign students. In fact, India considered the provision of higher education to the citizens as a national responsibility at the time of independence and extended full support to all institutions of higher education including the privately established ones.

When education is considered as a national investment, it is higher education and not school level education that one should take into consideration, though school level education is the prerequisite for higher education. Universal school education can at best help in creating an enlightened society but higher education is the ultimate infrastructure for all kinds of human resource development. As the Task Force on Higher Education and Society of the World Bank notes, "Higher Education simultaneously improves individual lives and enriches wider society, indicating a substantial overlap between private and public interests in higher education. Higher education raises wages and productivity, which makes both individuals and countries richer. It allows people to enjoy an enhanced 'life of the mind', offering wider society both cultural and political benefits. And it can encourage independence and initiative, both valuable commodities in the knowledge society." (World Bank, 2000) But now, in order to restrict spending on education, there seems to be an attempt to distinguish primary education from higher education stating that primary education is a merit item for subsidy and higher education is a non-merit item and this trend needs to be checked.

2.3 Increasing Demand for Non-formal and Life-long Learning

The explosion of knowledge and development in Science and Technology has resulted in the need for skilled personnel for all kinds of jobs. This has dictated the need for development of newer skills among the workforce. All the adults will have to keep up with the growing new knowledge and skills, by resorting to continuing education. A learning society will emerge in the next couple of decades in which there will be more adults going to educational institutions than they are now. They may demand a flexible educational structure with high levels of diversification. The employment sector has also started looking at human resource development as an investment. All this has resulted in the need for *life long learning* which demands flexibility in the mode of learning to suit the differential characteristic of the mature and adult learners. The implication is that the institutions of higher education should plan for more skill oriented courses in flexible modes of learning. All the colleges and universities will have to participate directly in providing the non-formal education and not leave them to some other agencies to take care of.

The Indian higher education system has responded to this trend by introducing job oriented courses and skill development courses, and by initiating distance and open education modes of delivery. Distance and open education are no longer considered the poor cousins of formal education. The annual enrolment in open universities in India has grown many folds. From 1994-95 to 1997-98 it recorded an increase from 2,00,939 to 3,50,000, a percentage increase of 74 per cent. Similarly the cumulative enrolment virtually doubled from 5,71,983 in 1995 to 10,50,000 in 1998, a percentage increase of 84 per cent. Correspondence course institutes have also witnessed considerable growth in student numbers. The cumulative enrolment was 8,50,000 in the year 1997-98 compared to 5,50,000 in the year 1994-95, a percentage increase of 55 per cent. (Khan, 1999) Today, 20 per cent of the students in higher education are being catered to through the distance mode. (Powar *et al.*, 2000b)

2.4 Political and Socio-economic Changes

The increasing economic integration across the world is one of the important changes the system of higher education has to deal with. There has been an increasing trend in the organisation of industrial or other production systems on a global scale rather than on national or regional scale. It means that these systems take the whole world as their market. Consequently, their activities including the acquisition of raw materials, services and other inputs will also be from around the world. In addition to this, there has also been a trend towards the formation of cross border alliances and ventures for the obvious advantage of much larger capital generation and for pooling the know how and resources to get the leading edge in the competitive market. Most of the nations now encourage free trade and have reduced the trade protection measures they were originally obsessed with. Any set of major corporations now enjoy complete freedom to locate their operations and research facilities anywhere in the world. This has brought high quality, relevant higher education to the key position in attracting global corporations because of the skills and knowledge such operations look for in the local workforce.

2.5 Increasing Private Initiatives

The need to increase the higher education provision along with the decreasing government support has resulted in encouraging the private initiatives in higher education. In the very recent period, growth of private engineering and medical colleges has been remarkable. The private higher education (PHE) institutions charge higher fee to meet the educational cost. While the public funded colleges are non-profit institutions, many of the private initiatives not merely cover their costs, but also make profits, which are not necessarily re-invested in education. The government policy is to encourage private initiatives in higher education but not commercialisation. (Joshi, M.M., 1998)

Private Higher Education institutions have come up in large numbers since the early 1980s and now they outnumber the public institutions in many of the thirty states in India. There are two categories of PHE institutions operating now. In one category are what are designated as self-financing institutions that function under the broad framework of similar public institutions in every respect except for the funding sources. They are affiliated to a public university of the region and thus are under the academic regulation of a university. They are by far the largest category and small trusts or individuals run them. Of the 12600 colleges of the country, nearly one-third are self-financing and most of them were established during the last 10-15 years. In the other category are institutions supported by a couple of corporate groups with a nationwide network of supporting institutions and teaching centres; but offering only diplomas and certificates and they remain outside the mainstream of formal institutions. A typical example is the NIIT group of institutions. By law they can't award degrees but they are successful in attracting students through the quality of their programmes and training.

The spread of self-financing colleges in the country is not even. In the southern states like Andhra Pradesh, Tamil Nadu, Karnataka and Maharashtra, the self-financing colleges are far more in number than the public ones; such is not the case in North India. The growth pattern of PHE institutions in one of the southern states, Andhra Pradesh indicates the general trend. In this state there were only 50 undergraduate public colleges in 1956. The number of colleges rose to 801 by 1996-97 and 989 by 2000-2001. Out of 989 colleges, 176 are directly established and funded by the government, 172 are aided (more than 95 per cent support from the government) colleges and 641 are private colleges. It is obvious that private colleges are far more in number than the government and aided colleges put together.

Likewise, if one looks at the growth of professional institutions, particularly the colleges of engineering, the extent of PHE prevalent in the country will be obvious. Andhra Pradesh had only 27 engineering colleges, both in the government and private sectors in 1990. The number of engineering colleges in the subsequent years are: 27 in 1991-92, 32 in 1995-96, 57 in 1996-97, 89 in 1997-98, 102 in 1998-99 and 105 in 2000-2001. Out of the 105 engineering colleges functioning currently, only 12 are public and the remaining 93 come under the PHE system.

In Tamil Nadu, yet another state in south India where PHE flourish, out of the 463 general education colleges, 228 are public funded and 235 are self-financing. The number of self-financing professional colleges is much more than the number of general education colleges. This pattern is also true for other professional undergraduate institutions for medicine, management, law, education, etc.

The existing public universities and colleges are encouraged to have programmes that are essentially self-financing and for which no government grants will be available. This initiative was taken for mobilizing additional resources for public institutions. Some of the universities and colleges offer as much as 60 to 70 per cent of their academic programmes under the self-financing scheme. This makes these public institutions hybrid systems having the characteristics of both private and public institutions. Both the central and state governments officially promote this trend.

With the experience of the failed public enterprises in many sectors, privatisation of higher education is viewed as a strategy to reach higher levels of competitive efficiency. Though this leads to higher financial implications to students and parents, those who pay for the benefits of the educational service of those institutions will make judgment about its quality or worthiness and only those institutions that pass this test of social accreditation will be able to survive. In the years to come these institutions will become more and more competitive in providing quality education and they will also grow to a much larger proportion than what is now, in comparison to the governmental and grant-in-aid institutions.

The other important economic change that has contributed to this trend is the improvement in the family finances. The size of the middle and upper income groups is on the increase in the socio-economic scene, indicating that the families would be able to contribute and invest in the education of their wards. According to an estimate, about 20 per cent of Indian households are as rich as their counterparts in Western Europe and for courses in demand families are ready to pay a high tuition fee. All these will result in the formation of a new compact in which the students, their families and the society along with the government will contribute collectively to the educational institutions, thus mutually helping each other and benefiting from each other. In other words the idea of self-financing institutions will gain greater acceptance and even become a predominant group in a decade or two.

2.6 Increasing Influence of Market Forces

Another major consideration that will have far-reaching implications is the changing trend in the labour market. It is also anticipated that, the overall trend in future will be, the decrease in the primary and manufacturing sector and increase in the employment scope in the service area. One could see that in the years to come there will be a large scale rise in the proportion of women who are economically active competing in the labour market more aggressively than before. There will also be an increase in the part time workers in the total work force as compared to the past. Gone are the days in which the unskilled labour force was considered as an asset. Now the market force demands workforce with specific knowledge and skills and this will have a great impact on the nature and content of higher education.

The third trend focuses on the growing importance given to Science and Technology, the nature of growth and development of knowledge domains and the changing role expectations of universities.

Trend III

3.1 Focus on Science and Technology (S&T)

An analysis of the amount spent on S&T, technical education and national facilities will stand evidence for this trend. Having understood the role of Research and Development (R&D) in the country's prosperity, the government has always been the major source of funding. In the first plan the allocation to research and development was 20 crores which increased to 17,529 crores in the Eighth Plan. Though the contribution of the private sector was negligible in the 60s, it has increased to an appreciable but inadequate percentage in 90s. The contribution of the private sector was 3.55 per cent in 1965-66 and it increased to 17 per cent in 1995-96. The quantum of fund may look impressive, but India doesn't spend even 1 per cent of GNP on R&D in science and technology while the developed countries spend between 2 per cent to 3 per cent of GNP.

Further, major portion of the fund of both states and central governments go for the funding of applied and experimental researches. Basic research receives only 12 per cent and 19 per cent of the total funding of R&D in science and technology from both the Governments respectively. The implication is that the institutions of higher education, whose primary concern and expertise is the basic research, should look in for more inputs from private initiatives. The university-industry linkage should be strengthened to bring in more resources for R&D.

A cursory look at the non-plan allocation of funds by Ministry of Human Resource Development (MHRD) for the year 1994-95, (which does not include the States' Plan and Non-Plan provisions and the 8th Plan provisions of the Centre) reveals that, every student in technical institutions is provided with funds as high as 13-fold of the per capita allocation in the general universities. As much as 14 per cent of the total education budget is spent on training a couple of hundred thousand students while apportioning only a meagre amount for the general higher education that caters to about 8 million students with about three and a half lakhs of teachers.

The focus on S&T can also be seen in the government's support to national facilities. India has various national laboratories outside the university system. The best of available human and monetary resources have been consequently diverted to these national laboratories. Though this was started with the laudable intention of fostering research in S&T, it has deprived the universities of being major partners in generating new knowledge.

3.2 Shift from Mono- to Multi- and Inter-disciplinarity

This trend is due to the knowledge explosion as well as assimilation and application of new inventions of science and technology in all walks of life. Throughout the world academia has not been slow to recruit knowledge from several sources when the outcome could serve either an academic or an economic purpose and as a result one can see a proliferation of inter- and multi-disciplinary areas of knowledge. Examples of inter- and multi-disciplinary work abound virtually every subject area. Biology was invaded by physics to create molecular biology. History requires anthropological, sociological, economic, legal conceptualisation in its different areas. The study of modern languages ranges from linguistics with its sociological and psychological contributions, to history and geography.

Although the formal definition of 'Disciplines' may be restrictive, many of the highest academic prizes go to those who do cross boundaries and the research councils have made inter-disciplinarity a priority of several of their initiatives. Disciplines are hard won formulations of sequences of concepts and evidence, which are reiteratively advanced through testing. By contrast, inter- and multi-disciplinary studies are domain based which do not start from development within disciplines but from problem areas, which may need knowledge from a whole range of disciplines for their solution. Medicine, planning social work and engineering are obvious examples. Such developments require thinking across several boundaries and making connections between them and higher education should be suitably structured to train the young minds for the same.

3.3 Rethinking the Role of Universities

The role of universities has been changing ever since the first university was established 900 and odd years ago at Bologna. Today, a university has multiple functions. The UNESCO report entitled "Learning: The Treasure Within" visualizes four functions for the universities:

> *First,* to prepare students for research and training,
> *Second,* to provide training courses oriented to the needs of society,
> *Third,* to be open to all to foster lifelong learning in its broadest sense, and
> *Fourth,* to strive for international cooperation.
>
> (UNESCO, 1996)

What was originally conceived, as a meeting place for intellectuals to deliberate, has become a mass education centre, down the centuries. Only after late 18th century, the responsibility of doing research for knowledge generation was added as a result of the influence of the German models. Not before the middle of this century, *i.e.* during the period of World War II and after, extension was part of the functions of the universities. Now the universities are expected not only to generate and transfer knowledge but also to provide extension services to transfer the benefits of knowledge. The inter-national dimension is also gaining significance now.

In India, too, the university is expected to be a place of learning and the sharing of knowledge, not only for those who enter its portals but also to those who, hitherto, have not benefited from the system. The UGC IX Plan stresses on this "third dimension" of education besides teaching and research, a policy adopted by it as early as 1977. It states in its chapter on "The University and Social Change", *The university can no longer confine itself to the classical model of education of producing graduates and post-graduates and undertaking research. The need of the hour is to move outside the confines of our walls and reach out to the community through extension education of groups who will never, otherwise, enter the university, or the college and through field action/outreach activities.* (UGC, IX Plan, 1996).

In line with the above statement, the UGC standing committee on adult education drafted the scheme entitled: "Adult, Continuing Education, Extension and Field Outreach",

2 Quality Concern

A Retrospect

In India, promoting quality in education has been the focus of almost all the committees constituted at different stages of the development of the higher education system. Among the various national consultations, discussions, and recommendations that gave a direction and focus to the developmental strategies after independence, the National Policies on Education (NPE) have played a major role. It is the NPE-1986 that made an explicit mention of the quality assurance mechanism that is needed for the Indian higher education. As an outcome of the NPE and its Programme of Action-1986, series of efforts were taken to put in place a quality assurance mechanism suitable for the Indian higher education system. This chapter focuses on those developments.

The National Policy on Education of 1968 marked a significant step in the development of the Indian higher education system by laying stress on the need for a radical reconstruction of the education system, to improve its quality at all stages. Since the adoption of the 1968 policy, there has been considerable expansion in educational facilities all over the country at all levels. While the expansion of the system of higher education has been impressive, the other general formulations incorporated in the 1968 policy did not, however, get translated into expected outcomes. As a result, problems of access, quality, utility, financial outlay and the others continued to get accumulated over the years and assumed such massive proportions that they had to be tackled without any further delay. This ushered in the New Education Policy of 1986. (GoI, NPE 1986)

Quality Concerns

Meanwhile, the growing concern for the quality of education at all the levels brought in the compulsion to make the Constitutional Amendment of 1976, to bring education into the Concurrent List so that the federal government can have a meaningful role to ensure quality of education. Until then, education remained as the responsibility of the state governments. This important amendment required the sharing of responsibility of maintaining the standard of education by the Union Government and the States. While the role and the responsibility of the States remain essentially unchanged, the Union Government has a larger role to play after the inclusion of education into the concurrent list. It has to reinforce the national and integrative character of education, maintain quality and standards, and monitor the educational requirements of the country as a whole. This includes the needs of research and advanced study, the international aspects of education, culture and Human Resource Development and, in general, to promote excellence at all levels of the educational pyramid.

In addition to the yet-to-be-tackled problems identified by the 1968 policy on education as listed earlier, the New Education Policy had to take note of other national concerns such as that education is essentially for all and it is a unique investment in the present and the future. Consequently, the policy document emphasised that, up to a specified level, all students irrespective of caste, creed, location and gender, have access to education of a comparable quality. While this aspect of the national policy is mostly related to the school education, the changing context the world over has brought in the additional responsibility of extending it to higher education also. From Universal Elementary Education the country has to move towards Universal Higher Education of a comparable quality.

The National Education Policy of 1986 was thus oriented towards giving effect to this meaningful and challenging partnership between the state and federal governments in letter and spirit. Consequently, the policy document has been concentrating on quality — excellence and relevance — throughout and has evolved a series of strategic plans to achieve the same. Expressing the concern about the quality, it advocates the development of co-ordinated methods to keep a watch on standards by the UGC and the State Councils. Under the section 'Improvement in efficiency', the policy notes a few major steps, which include the following two, which have a direct bearing on institutional evaluation as an effective method for monitoring the accountability and quality issues:

— Excellence in performance of institutions and individuals will be recognised and rewarded. The emergence of substandard institutions will be checked. A climate conducive to excellence and innovation will be promoted with full involvement of the faculty.

— Select institutions will be awarded academic, administrative and financial autonomy of varying degrees, building in safeguards — with respect to accountability. (GoI, NPE 1986)

Under the section, 'To make the system work', the policy document identified that the strategy would consist of creation of a system of performance appraisals of institutions according to standards and norms set at the National or State levels. In sum, the focus of NPE-1986 was to ensure and assure quality of education combined with accountability. The best and perhaps the only method to achieve these twin objectives is to assess the performance of institutions and guide them towards improvement. This process of institutional evaluation would bring out the strengths and weaknesses of the institutions and that could be the basis for improving the total quality of the education system as a whole. Therefore, this was considered to be the ideal instrument for ensuring accountability as well as for promoting quality in education.

Appreciating the importance of such a quality assuring mechanism, both the National Policy on Education and the Programme of Action (PoA), 1986 *inter alia* recommended the establishment of a National Accreditation body. In fact the PoA had clearly spelt out the scope and nature of such a body in the following statements:

> "Excellence of institutions of higher education is a function of many aspects: self-evaluation and self-improvement are important among them. If a mechanism is set up which will encourage self-assessment in institutions and also assessment and accreditation by a Council of which these institutions are corporate members, the quality of process, participation, achievements, etc. will be constantly monitored and improved" (GoI, PoA, 1986)

Establishment of the Quality Assurance Body

In view of the above directives of NPE/PoA, the University Grants Commission (UGC) of India constituted a 15-member Committee on Accreditation and Assessment Council under the Chairmanship of Dr. Vasant Gowarikar, Secretary, Ministry of Science and Technology, Government of India. The terms of reference of the committee were to *make recommendations regarding setting up of Accreditation and Assessment Council in order to develop a mechanism for maintenance and raising of quality of institutions of higher education while keeping in view the objectives, uses and various methods/procedures that are currently being followed by different countries or that can be adopted.* (UGC, 1987)

This committee constituted a sub-committee under the convenership of Dr. Vasant Gowarikar to bring out a working paper on the above terms of reference. After a great deal of discussions on various aspects of assessment and accreditation of educational institutions a working group was set-up. The responsibility of the working group was to prepare a draft document suggesting practical steps towards setting up of the Assessment and Accreditation Council indicating the objectives, functions, structure and methodology of assessing the performance of educational institutions. The working group submitted the draft to the sub-committee who placed the same before the main committee on 9th December 1987. The main committee accepted the draft and submitted it to UGC.

The report dealt with the following aspects:

(*a*) Aspects of management of higher education and its shortcomings,
(*b*) Process of accreditation, its objects and methodology of working,
(*c*) Assessment of institutional effectiveness in each of the principal areas of institutional activity and responsibility,
(*d*) Steps towards an accreditation system in India and how to organize the process, and
(*e*) Linkages with other accrediting agencies and development of the National Test Service.

The UGC considered the report of the Committee on Accreditation and Assessment Council and decided that:

(*a*) The report be widely circulated among the academics,
(*b*) Regional seminars and a national seminar be convened to discuss the report and
(*c*) The comments of the academics along with the recommendations of the seminars may be placed before the Commission.

Subsequently, the report of the committee was deliberated in nine regional seminars held at universities of Andhra, Annamalai, Gauhati, Kalyani, Lucknow, Mysore, Pune, Punjab and Rajasthan and at the national level seminar held at Jawaharlal Nehru University, New Delhi. Except for the two workshops organised at Kalyani and Gauhati Universities, all others strongly favoured the development of a system for assessment and accreditation of institutions of higher education under the auspices of the UGC. The national seminar also reiterated that the accreditation system should enjoy reasonable autonomy in its structure and functioning. The seminar further suggested that the new system should be set-up in such a way as to get maximum acceptance and credibility.

Based on the consensus arrived at the national and other regional deliberations, the UGC requested Dr. A. Sukumaran Nair, former Pro-Vice-Chancellor, University of Kerala to submit a project report on National Accreditation Board for Higher Education (NABHE). The report submitted in December 1990 contained comments on the following:

(*a*) The Gowarikar's report,
(*b*) The concept of accreditation,
(*c*) Major functions of accreditation,
(*d*) Objectives and functions of the accreditation system in the Indian context,
(*e*) Management of accreditation system, its administrative and organizational pattern,
(*f*) Linkages with professional bodies, and
(*g*) Modalities of accreditation and rating scale to be used for assessing institutions.

The report also dealt with the accountability of NABHE to UGC and the financial implication of the process. (Nair, S., 1990)

In a parallel effort, but with the specific agenda to review the management patterns and to set criteria for assessment of performance of educational institutions, UGC appointed a Committee in January 1987 under the Convenership of Professor A. Gnanam, then Vice-Chancellor of the Bharathidasan University (the Vice-Chancellor, University of Madras when the report was submitted). The committee recommended that performance of an academic institution should be evaluated at least after every three years, by autonomous bodies comprising of experts. The report of the committee entitled "Report of the UGC Committee Towards New Educational Management" and popularly known as Gnanam Committee report, noted: "We feel that the deficiency of the present system of management is the absence of any systematic method of reporting and evaluation of performance of the university. The society has invested precious resources in building up the great institutions of higher learning. It is entitled to demand that the members of the academic community individually and collectively be made accountable in concrete visible terms." (UGC, 1990) The report spelt out in detail the criteria for assessment and how the performance evaluation should be done — assigning weightages to criteria, scoring and classification of institutions into five grades that range from A (80 per cent and above — Outstanding) to F (below 30 per cent — very poor).

Policy Revision in 1992

Meanwhile, the National Policy on Education underwent substantial revision. The revised policy document (1992) also accentuated the need to effect an all-round improvement in the institutions and proposed that the main emphasis should be on the consolidation and expansion of facilities in the existing institutions. It laid stress on the need to take urgent steps to protect the system from degradation. To make the system work, the strategy identified in the policy document 1986 on performance appraisal of institutions was reiterated. In March 1992, based on the outcome of the earlier efforts in this regard, UGC resolved to set up a National Accreditation Board as an autonomous body for the achievement of the objectives envisaged in the NPE.

The Memorandum of Association and Rules and Regulations of the accreditation body were submitted to UGC in January 1994. The UGC towards the end of July 1994, constituted an empowered committee under the chairmanship of Prof. G. Ram Reddy, Chairman, UGC to finalise the memorandum of association and rules and regulation of the accreditation board. The document prepared after taking into consideration the existing methods of quality assessment and quality control of higher education in USA, UK, Canada, Australia and also the higher education scenario in India, was considered by the empowered committee and was approved on September 7, 1994. It culminated in the establishment of the body with the name *National Assessment and Accreditation Council* (NAAC).

The Functioning of NAAC

The PoA document specifically suggested that the new Council to be established, should enjoy reasonable autonomy in its functioning. The mode of operation of the proposed body, as suggested in the PoA, reads as follows:

> "As a part of its responsibility for the maintenance and promotion of standards of education, the UGC will, to begin with, take the initiative to establish the Accreditation and Assessment Council as an autonomous body. It will evolve its own criteria and methodology for accreditation and assessment. Its main functions will be catalytic: it will analyse and evaluate institutions and their performance to facilitate self-improvement. This Council will be supported by a professional secretariat in the performance of its functions." (GoI, PoA, 1992)

In line with this recommendation NAAC was established as an autonomous body, under Section 12-CCC of UGC Act, 1956, registered under Karnataka Societies Registration Act of 1960 and Karnataka Societies Registration Rules of 1961 at Bangalore on September 16, 1994. Its working is controlled by the General Council (GC) and the Executive Committee (EC) on which organisations such as UGC, AICTE, MHRD, Association of Indian Universities (AIU), Universities, professional bodies, senior academics and educational administrators are represented. In the first GC of NAAC there were eleven members and by 1996, NAAC had its full GC of 35 members drawn from different sectors of higher education, to steer its policy decisions. The Chairman of UGC is the

President of the General Council of NAAC. The Chairperson of EC is a senior academic. The Executive Officer of NAAC is the Director, with the status of a Central University Vice-Chancellor, who is its academic and administrative head, and is the member secretary of both GC and EC. NAAC has a core staff and consultants. In addition it takes help from a large number of academics and educational administrators.

Roles and Responsibilities of NAAC

The objective of NAAC as envisaged in the revised Memorandum of Association (MoA) of 2000 is to assess and accredit institutions of higher learning in India, universities and colleges or one or more of their units, *i.e.* departments, schools, institutions, programmes, etc. The main objectives of assessment and accreditation are to:

- Grade institutions of higher education and their programmes
- Stimulate the academic environment and quality of teaching and research in these institutions
- Help institutions realise their academic objectives
- Promote necessary changes, innovations and reforms in all aspects of the institutions working for the above purpose
- Encourage innovations, self-evaluation and accountability in higher education

The MoA also stated that assessment and accreditation is to be based on the following criteria:

- Institutional mission and objectives
- Organisation and governance
- Infrastructural facilities
- Quality of teaching and learning
- Curriculum design and review
- Support services
- Student services

— Sources, adequacy and management of financial resources
— Publications and consultancy/extension activities
— Any other aspect the Executive Committee of NAAC would like to examine

NAAC shall ensure that the criteria are:

— Reviewed periodically and revised and updated as and when considered necessary in the light of experience gained through their application and development of the techniques and modalities of assessment,
— Objective and, to the extent possible, quantifiable, and
— Publicise widely, particularly, in the academic community.

NAAC shall:

— Arrange for the periodic assessment and grading of institutions of higher education, or units thereof, or specific academic programmes or projects.
— Communicate the results of assessment and grading to the concerned institution in a form and manner appropriate for corrective action, rectification and self-improvement.
— Help and encourage the institutions in developing their own procedures, techniques and modalities for self-evaluation.
— Initiate research studies, in planning and evaluation of educational institutions, programmes etc.
— Ensure an optimised use of resources and the achievement of the identified goals of institutions of higher learning.
— Establish regional branches as and when necessary to ensure the smooth conduct of assessment and accreditation. (MoA of NAAC, 2000)

In fulfilling its role NAAC aspires to be a catalytic agency to motivate institutions of higher learning to achieve excellence in all spheres of academic activity. It strives to promote the idea of accountability without the fear of punitive action. The philosophy of NAAC is ameliorative and enabling rather than punitive or judgmental.

The Process

An analysis of the current practices of the national accrediting agencies of the different countries reveals a great deal of diversity. They vary in structure and function. Variations could be seen in their methodology and also outcome. In spite of the variance, world over, the process of External Quality Assurance (EQA) is a combination of the self-study report of the institution and peer review. This is the accepted methodology of all national agencies that are members of the International Network for Quality Assurance Agencies in Higher Education (INQAAHE). In line with the international trend, the National Assessment and Accreditation Council follows the following three-stage process for accrediting a unit of assessment:

— Preparation and submission of self-study report by the unit of assessment
— On-site visit of the peer team for validation of the report
— Final decision by the Executive Council of NAAC

The first and the most important step in the process of assessment and accreditation is the preparation of the self-study report by the institution along the guidelines formulated by NAAC. The self-study report is expected to project the functioning of the institution with respect to the seven criteria for assessment given below:

— Curricular Aspects
— Teaching-learning and Evaluation
— Research, Consultancy and Extension
— Infrastructure and Learning Resources

— Student Support and Progression
— Organisation and Management
— Healthy Practices

On receiving the self-study report from the institution, a visiting team is constituted by NAAC, to validate the self-study report by an on-site visit. The visit expands from 3 to 5 days depending on the size and complexity of the unit to be assessed. Towards the fag end of the visit, the team discusses the issues of concern that find a place in the assessment report, with the head of the institution, for observation and reaction. Through this interaction, any discrepancies and gaps in information are eliminated. The report, without the confidential part, is shared with the institution and the oral feedback on the highlights of the same is disclosed to the representatives of the institution during the exit meeting.

The validation and the subsequent assessment lead to an overall institutional grade and a detailed report, which begins with the team agreeing on the criterion-wise scores. Taking cognizance of the variance in types of institutions, the seven criteria for assessment have been allotted differential weightages. The weightages marked below are used for calculating the institutional score:

Table 5: Criteria and Weightages

Criteria	*University*	*Affiliated/ Constituent Colleges*	*Autonomous Colleges*
Curricular Aspects	15	10	15
Teaching–learning and Evaluation	25	40	30
Research, Consultancy and Extension	15	05	10
Infrastructure and Learning Resources	15	15	15
Student Progression and Support	10	10	10
Organisation and Management	10	10	10
Healthy Practices	10	10	10

The weighted average of the scores is calculated applying the following formula:

$$\text{Institutional score} = \Sigma\, C_i W_i \;/\; \Sigma\, W_i \;(\, i = 1, 2, \ldots, 7)$$

where W_i = weightage of the ith criterion and C_i = score of the ith criterion. The institutional score is further used by NAAC to get the overall grade. If the overall score is not less than 55 per cent, the institution gets the *Accredited* status. The accredited institutions are graded on a nine-point scale with the following scale values:

Table 6: Institutional Scores (Upper Limit Exclusive) and Grades

Grade	*Institutional score*
A^{++}	95-100
A^{+}	90-95
A	85-90
B^{++}	80-85
B^{+}	75-80
B	70-75
C^{++}	65-70
C^{+}	60-65
C	55-60

Institutions, which do not attain the minimum 55 per cent points for accreditation, would also be intimated and notified indicating that the institution is "ASSESSED AND FOUND NOT QUALIFIED FOR ACCREDITATION". After EC's decision the overall grade along with the criterion-wise scores is informed to the institution and the information is included in the web site. Once the language editing is over, the detailed report that highlights the strengths and weaknesses of the institution under various criteria is put on the NAAC web site. At every stage of firming up the methodology detailed above, a large number of academia has been involved and the international practices have been analysed.

The national level consultation of eight years that preceded the establishment of NAAC gave a strong base to NAAC to build its functions. The field experience of the next eight years has enabled NAAC to fine-tune its criteria for assessment and grading system to suit the Indian soil, making the process of assessment and accreditation a truly Indian model. In the course of development, NAAC faced many challenges that were overcome with the support of the higher education institutions and the academia who were convinced of the merits of EQA and the developments are discussed in the following chapters.

3 Relevance of Assessment and Accreditation

In the initial stages, the Indian higher education institutions hesitated to volunteer for accreditation by NAAC. There may be several reasons for hesitation on the part of these institutions to come forward for external assessment. Besides the general inertia and the fear of getting assessed by others, there may also be a lingering doubt in the minds of some about the relevance of the entire concept of assessment and accreditation to the Indian context. But today, when assessment and accreditation has become the order of the day the world over, and when more than 100 countries of good standing have already established their own national councils for ensuring the quality of their higher education, there is no place to harp on the old skepticism. An attempt is made in this chapter to remove such apprehensions in the minds of the academia and to indicate the relevance and importance of assessment and accreditation to the country now more than ever.

The establishment of NAAC for quality assurance in higher

education has been a significant move in Indian higher education. NAAC was aware that for the success of any national strategy, consensus building and broad involvement are very important. During the first three years, till 1997, NAAC evolved through a series of consultative interactions with a large body of academia, norms, methods and a series of instruments for assessment and accreditation. Among the norms, it was decided that NAAC should concentrate on institutions as the unit of assessment, with provision for assessing individual departments also, and the accreditation should be a voluntary process.

During the first year of operationalising the instruments and methodology, during 1998-99, 30 institutions of higher education — 3 universities and 27 colleges, were assessed. Following this, there has definitely been an increasing response to NAAC's call. Yet it has a long way to go to complete even the first round of its mission. As of December 2002, seventy out of about 160 universities and 226 out of about 12,600 colleges that come under the purview of liberal arts and science education have been accredited. In spite of the extensive effort taken to disseminate NAAC's mission and its role through a number of awareness activities, it appears that many institutions are still hesitant to come forward to get assessed.

Reservations

It is well understood that without value added human resource — value addition through higher education — no country can flourish in the competitive world. Therefore, there is a premium on both quantity and quality of higher education; *Quantity* in terms of increased access to higher education to the level of at least 40 per cent to 50 per cent of relevant age group and *Quality* in terms of relevance and excellence of the academic programmes offered.

In the past fifty years, India, along with other countries of the world, has been concentrating on the quantitative expansion of higher educational network and understandably did not pay adequate attention to the quality in any concerted way beyond the internal checks and balances that one does in any institutional organisational set-up. Now, because of the quantum change in the socio-economic context the world over, the quality of education has become crucial. This concern for quality has made everyone focus on ways of ensuring quality of education offered both by existing institutions and the new ones to be established. Though the quality of education to be offered by the new institutions could hopefully be ensured through regulatory processes, it is difficult to apply the same strategy for the existing ones. The best way to do this is to evaluate the performance of the existing institutions by identifying their strengths and weaknesses to begin with. In fact, this is in a way a *SWOT* analysis for the educational institutions — understanding ones own Strengths, Weaknesses, Opportunities and Threats which is similar to what has been found useful in improving the efficiency of the performance of industrial houses.

The need for this kind of assessment — a performance appraisal — of institutions has been felt by the educational planners and policy makers for a long time which culminated into the establishment of NAAC as the national apex body and a few others for the professional education sector. The speciality councils such as Medical Council of India (MCI) and Dental Council of India (DCI) are evolving their own strategies for ensuring quality of the professional programmes. Thus, the once misunderstood and feared, performance evaluation through the external assessment process is now seen as an instrument of ensuring quality in education and is used extensively world over.

Oblivious of all that is happening around the world, a few skeptics have expressed their reservation about the role and relevance of NAAC. Their views are based on wrong perceptions about the functioning of higher education institutions, global context and other compelling imperatives. Some of the arguments in favour of their reservations on EQA by NAAC are as follows:

- While Universities are established by an Act of

Parliament or State Legislatures and also controlled by Central or State Governments, is there any need for an external quality assurance agency like NAAC?

- While the UGC has the authority to ensure standards of education, why do we need NAAC?
- Will NAAC's work not lead to duplication of work done by AIU in some aspects like ensuring equivalence of degrees?
- Do we need NAAC's process when universities have their own monitoring mechanisms for their affiliated institutions and for themselves?
- Will assessment and accreditation be meaningful in the affiliating mode of the Indian system of education?
- Will it not be enough if the existing structures for monitoring higher education — the UGC and the University mechanisms — are made to function more effectively, instead of establishing another agency like NAAC resulting in duplication of functions?
- Universities have the authority to award degrees and their equivalence is already agreed upon. Will not the balance be affected adversely by NAAC's methodology of assessment and accreditation and consequent grading?
- How do the institutions of higher learning stand to gain by NAAC's assessment and accreditation except for their being graded?
- Will not NAAC's assessment demoralise institutions that do not perform well?
- What will happen to students and teachers of institutions that do not perform well in NAAC's assessment?
- Is it worth trying this American model on the Indian system of education?

One category of apprehensions relates to the government control, UGC's mandate, AIU's role and the various other monitoring mechanisms that are already in practice in the system and hence the question, *Do we need another agency like*

NAAC? The government control, directly or indirectly, looks into the need for the eligibility criteria to establish institutions, and fitness of the established ones to receive support. Even in other countries, no degree awarding post-secondary educational institution is established without some kind of governmental regulation or parliamentary/legislative channels. Consequently corresponding mechanisms to check their viability and performance are built-in. Admittedly, these measures are meant only to take care of the minimal functions and not to maximise the quality of education. All that the government and other semi-governmental agencies can do is to oversee the monitoring mechanisms through financial and academic audit and satisfy themselves that minimal performance has taken place and nothing more. UGC, as a funding body, has been doing the same while supporting the institutions.

But the frame of reference for assessment and accreditation by NAAC is excellence in education and not minimal standard. The outcome of the process will indicate whether an institution is *Good, Average* or *Not Satisfactory* from the point of view of quality education. As the process needs to be undertaken with utmost care and in a systematic and scientific way, UGC has established NAAC as an autonomous body with financial support.

In contrast, AIU is an Association of all the universities/university level institutions that have some basic infrastructure and student strength. Once an institution becomes a member there is nothing in the scheme of AIU to assess it periodically and monitor the quality of the education offered. As a service to the member institutions, AIU checks the equivalence in course content of any programme offered by an institution so that student mobility is facilitated among the institutions. The process involves the certification that the courses are equivalent but does not make any quality assessment of the education provided by its member institutions. On the other hand, NAAC's process is comprehensive and a holistic way of judging the institutional functioning and the quality of education offered therein.

There is also a question that while universities have their own monitoring mechanisms for their affiliated institutions and for themselves, why do they need NAAC's process. It is true to some extent that there are certain mechanisms already existing in every university, and university level institutions to ensure quality. Various important bodies like the Executive Council, Court or Senate, Planning Board, Academic Council and Boards of Studies are meant to ensure quality. Despite the assumption that these bodies function efficiently, there is a danger in accepting their adequacy. The reason being that, each body has its own specific and distinct sphere of responsibility and consequently total quality in education is not the prime agenda of any single body. The holistic approach that is essential for meaningful evaluation is also neglected. Further, the internal mechanisms will not withstand the test of objectivity at the national and international levels and it is NAAC's process that will solve this problem. In a nutshell, the roles of government, UGC, AIU and the internal mechanisms of the institutions do not overlap with NAAC's process, as the frame of reference for each body is distinctly different from that of NAAC.

Some are doubtful whether assessment and accreditation will be meaningful in the affiliating mode of Indian system. In fact, it is in the affiliating mode, where quality becomes no one's concern, that assessment and accreditation gains significance. The affiliating mode is not a system unique to India. It is in vogue in other countries of the Indian subcontinent and also in a few commonwealth countries. To some extent even UK has some form of an affiliating mode of dispensing higher education. They call it *franchising* the educational modules that constitute the curriculum. Whether a particular country adopts the affiliating mode or a unitary mode of institutional functioning, there have always been accrediting systems for the professional programmes. The Medical Council, Bar Council and Pharmacy Council have been functioning all along and they have no problem of functioning in the prevailing context in India or elsewhere. While the other speciality councils cater to only 15 per cent of the student population, NAAC is meant for the whole system with 85 per cent of the student population from the liberal arts and science streams who are not covered by any speciality councils. The experience of other councils indicates that there is no reason to doubt the meaningful functioning of NAAC in the existing system.

While there are queries about the relevance in the affiliating mode, there is also a concern about what will happen to students and teachers of institutions that don't perform well in NAAC's process. NAAC's process aims at informing the beneficiaries where an institution stands so that students can make a right choice of institutions and the institutions can try to improve. There is already a force working in the system that recognises or derecognises the institutions for their merit or demerit, *viz.*, Social Accreditation. The MCI and AICTE have been recognizing and derecognising programmes and institutions back and forthwith no significant hardship to the students. In contrast, NAAC's process will serve the beneficiaries — Institutions, Students, Parents, Funding Agencies, Government and Industries, in aspects like internal management, evaluation of teaching and research activities, choice of institution, effective funding of research and development, institution-industry linkage and graduate employment. Further, in the context of emerging trends like internationalising education, education that crosses the national border and the active participation of private sector, NAAC's process can serve the international dimension of quality assurance and facilitate the stakeholders to make informed decisions.

Borrowed Model?

Finally, when all criticisms are exhausted, some take refuge in questioning the suitability of this "American model". Every country evolves a system not only by learning from its experiences but also by taking the experiences of others and continuously adjusting to its contextual and national demands. That is exactly the philosophy of sharing the know-how. NAAC has taken the experience of many other countries to evolve a system of its own to suit the Indian soil. It is as much British or

Philippine or Canadian as it is American. It is true that USA has been a pioneer in accreditation with a century long history, but the purposes accreditation serve in USA have already been realised by the affiliating functions of the Indian system. Therefore, when India had to launch the quality assurance strategy, a suitable model that would ensure quality and standards over and above the existing regulations had to be thought of. Towards that purpose, the elements that would work well in the Indian context have been incorporated into the NAAC's methodology.

While working towards the same purpose of quality assurance in higher education, similarity in certain dimensions cannot be avoided. In fact, to facilitate agreements between the quality assurance agencies of different countries, adhering to common critical elements becomes necessary. At the same time, the Indian model has not lost sight of the unique purposes it has to serve. So far NAAC has taken up institutional accreditation, where the whole institution becomes the unit of assessment. This is similar to the institutional accreditation carried out by the regional and national accreditation agencies of USA. But in terms of the criteria that form the basis for accreditation and the public disclosure of the assessment reports, NAAC follows a strategy, which is different from the American model. In US, the assessment reports are shared only with the institutions and as such they are not public documents. But in NAAC's methodology, making the assessment report public is a critical element.

NAAC's methodology differs from the UK model in terms of the overall grade, criteria for assessment and unit of assessment. In UK, the teaching quality assessment by the Quality Assurance Agency (QAA) looks at six aspects of the learning experience and its outcomes and the assessors award grades on a scale of 1-4 for each aspect, where 4 is the highest. Comments identifying good practice and areas for improvement are published in an assessment report. Reports are available from the QAA and on the HEFCE web site. The Research Assessment Exercise conducted every few years is based on publications, products or even artistic performances of the subjects, which are assessed through peer review by panels of experts in the subject and it does not require visit to the institutions. (HEFCE, 1998)

These are just a few examples to show how NAAC's process has both similarities and differences while compared to the methodology followed in other countries. In other words, one can be legitimately proud of the truly Indian model of external quality assurance.

The real picture of the response from the academia would be incomplete without a mention of the reactions of a few who have conviction on the relevance of NAAC. They wonder why such an enabling process has not been made mandatory. They question why the funding is yet to be linked with the outcome of assessment and accreditation. NAAC has been convincing them indicating that the stakeholders are already linking some of their funding decisions to assessment outcome and some higher education institutions might need some more time to tune up to the quality assurance developments. The objective of leading the institutions towards continuous quality improvement through a facilitating and ameliorative process cannot be achieved satisfactorily if it is linked directly to funding.

Normally, all institutions go through various stages of development and the ultimate stage of development is *aspiring for excellence* where the focus is not just the impression of the society but also the value judgment of an objective process. NAAC's process is directed towards this enlightened extreme. An institution that wishes to have a better understanding of its strengths and weaknesses through the peer assessment, an institution that wishes to inform its beneficiaries where it stands with reference to its avowed commitments to higher education will benefit from NAAC's process. Institutions need time to mature to that stage of submitting themselves for external scrutiny and, if made mandatory, the process will become a self-defeating mission. Nonetheless, the social pressure will make it almost a necessity in due course.

Anyone who follows the trends of the socio-economic changes and the consequent impact on the educational system in India will appreciate the relevance of NAAC. Even those who have been questioning the need for an agency like NAAC have been doing so because of their concern for the system. Academia have always been receptive to any move towards improving the system, provided they are convinced of the merits. The day is not far away when those who are yet to be convinced too would join others to strengthen the mission of quality in higher education.

Part II: Issues of Policy

The international scenario of the quality assurance agencies presents a diverse and rich picture. Some of them are established and supported by their respective governments. Others are either independent or quasi-government bodies and, in a few countries, they are formed as an institutional consortium. These bodies may undertake only the accreditation on a two-point scale or carry out an elaborate assessment and grade the units or restrict themselves to the overall academic audit without grading. Likewise many of them may confine assessment to the review of either teaching and learning or the research activities of the unit or do both. Other aspects of such variations could be seen in their methodology and using the assessment outcome for funding decisions. The reasons for this variation are many and, therefore, one cannot say which is the best. However, for a given frame of reference, it is possible to identify the best model that is most suitable for the national context. This part is an attempt to highlight how NAAC made policy decisions on those critical aspects – unit of assessment, grading system, and collaborating with other professional bodies. It also highlights how the other stakeholders are taking policy decisions to use assessment outcome for decision-making.

4 Unit of Assessment for Accreditation

One major aspect that needs careful attention is the choice of the "Unit" for assessment before a desirable model is evolved. Almost all countries have some mechanisms already in place, which would assess the institution as a whole. Some national assessment agencies use the individual academic programme as unit for assessment and a few others use a mixture of both. The choice seems to depend on many considerations. The size of the national system of higher education as a whole, the specific purpose for which the assessment has been commissioned, the significance of the outcomes to the stakeholders, its viability, and, above all, the feasibility of such reviews are some of them. This chapter discusses these considerations that have dictated the policy decision by NAAC to promote institutional accreditation in the first phase at the same time with the provision for departmental accreditation.

While evolving and operationalising quality assurance mechanisms, one may come across many issues, the relative level of importance of which will vary greatly. Some of the important issues that have a direct bearing on the choice of the unit for assessment are discussed below.

Coverage of the Agency

The coverage of the quality assurance agency is of foremost importance. The overall size of the higher educational network varies with the countries. The total number of students enrolled, and number of institutions involved are some of the factors that determine the size of the system. It ranges from a single University (Mauritius) to hundreds of them as in USA, Russia and India. India, which has the second largest network of higher education system, has 274 universities and about 12,600 colleges with more than 8 million students enrolled. Obviously, for any country that has a large sized educational system, choosing any unit smaller than the institution, will have many practical difficulties. If one chooses the department of study or the discipline as unit, the number of units to be assessed will run into a few hundreds or thousands, a stupendous and practically difficult job to be done within the normal assessment cycle of 4 to 5 years. In a country like UK, where there is a relatively smaller number of large institutions, the choice was made some years ago to use the programme as the unit of assessment for assessing teaching quality and two cycles have been completed so far. Even in UK, the institutional audit mechanisms co-exist. In India where there is a large number of smaller institutions, the institution happens to be the obvious choice. This has been the experience of many other countries also.

In Canada, education is a provincial responsibility and there is no 'national level' mechanism in place for quality assurance. In fact, some of the provinces follow 'quality assurance' procedures, quite similar to the 'affiliating functions' of India. At the provincial level, it is possible for them to focus on programmes. For example, the Ontario Council for Graduate Studies (OCGS) has only 17 universities in its membership and obviously programme level assessment is necessary for OCGS. In fact OCGS has two types of assessment — one for the already existing programmes and the other for the new programmes to be started. A committee of just 21 members does both the processes and this could be possible due to the limited number of units to be covered. (OCGS, 1996) The province of Alberta also has only 26 institutions of higher education — universities, colleges and technical schools across the province, and the institutions are assessed on key areas of performance at the institutional level.

Within the same country variation in approach could be seen as the size of the higher education of the province increases. The coverage of Commission on Evaluation of College Education (CEEC) of the Quebec province is relatively big with 117 institutions. This does not include the universities since they have a separate quality assurance mechanism. In 1997 when CEEC carried out the evaluation of Business Administration Technology programme, all the 49 general and vocational colleges funded by the ministry had been authorised to offer the same. In the private sector, out of the 59 colleges only seven subsidised colleges had the authorization to offer this programme. In other words, to cover the whole province with respect to a specific programme, CEEC had to evaluate 56 reports, which is still a manageable number. In the other rounds of evaluation, CEEC also assessed the aspects like student evaluation, general education component etc., but it was done at the institutional level and now CEEC has moved towards holistic institutional review. (CEEC, 1994, 1997)

Even in New Zealand and Hong Kong since the number of institutions to be covered is very low, programme level or aspect level assessment like assessment of Teaching-Learning Quality Review could be possible.

Collective Impact

Apart from the practical aspects, the use of an institution as a unit of assessment has many advantages. The academic quality is justifiably defined as, not the quality of individual teachers but the collective impact of an overall academic programme designed and delivered by the institution as a whole for providing the desired knowledge, skills and competencies. If it is true, as it is indeed, then the assessment strategy should focus on the *collective impact*. In that case, the institution will be the obvious choice as the unit of assessment because institutions are responsible for the introduction of programmes based on the current trends and changed expectations, and for the design and delivery of the courses. Individuals do contribute but they cannot do so without the academic soundness of the institution.

Centralised Facilities and Management

Only the institution can facilitate the multi-disciplinary and inter-disciplinary programmes through co-ordination among the various constituent departments of studies. The Choice Based Credit systems, which is an educational innovation being adopted by more and more institutions allows a lot of flexibility to students in constructing his/her own curriculum by choosing from a cafeteria of courses. For example, a student of Environmental Science may choose a combination wherein he would be taking courses from five different departments — Hindi, English, Chemistry, Botany and Environmental Science. Institutional arrangements have a major role in the success of such curricular transactions.

It is also the responsibility of the institutional management to provide the various infrastructure and learning resources such as central library, computer centres, residential halls, facilities for sports and games, cultural activities, academic activities like seminars, debating etc. These significantly contribute to the academic soundness of the programme.

Further, it is the responsibility of the institutions to provide the academic environment that helps in developing the general skills that fall beyond the realm of subject specialization and classroom teaching. Institutions act as the training ground for several skills such as communication, capacity to work in a team, citizenry and other expected or implicit maturity among the students. The ideal and rich corporate life of the many campuses generally provides opportunities for students to develop their inherent talents and the institutions are empowered to provide the needed rich ambiance in the campuses for this purpose. In fact the institution as a whole is responsible for providing all the implicit and explicit provisions for developing desired values and skills among students. Consequently only when the institution is assessed for its mission, objectives, policies, principles, processes and various inputs, one can get an insight into the quality of education offered.

That is why even the agencies that do programme accreditation give adequate attention to the institutional level arrangements. For example, the University Council of Jamaica (UCJ) effects programme accreditation; however a process of institutional assessment must precede accreditation of any programme in an institution. To be eligible for programme accreditation, institutions must first seek registration with the UCJ. The criteria for registration are closely related to the criteria for accreditation since they are meant to provide registered institutions with a foundation for logical development towards accreditation. A registered institution seeking UCJ's accreditation of its programmes must make application to the UCJ and conduct a self-study. The institution has to submit the completed application form detailing the programme accompanied by supplementary information about the programme and the institutional self-study. (UCJ, 1998)

Impact on Policies

The international experience also reveals that assessing the institution as a whole has made significant impact on policy related issues. The institutional level assessment triggers change in the system as procedural gaps are identified and that promotes policy level changes. Australia had three rounds of institutional audits during 1993 and 1995, which was found to have fostered and enhanced enduring awareness of the importance of internal quality assurance. Noting the impact of institutional audits, the Department of Education, Training and Youth Affairs notes, "Rather than providing a snapshot of current activities as the discipline reviews had, this holistic approach had the advantage of involving much of the universities in a self-analysis and it evaluated policy and hence commitment to the future." (DETYA, 2000)

Critical Mass

Although the situation may be different in the developed world, looking for the *critical size* of the unit is an important factor for undertaking assessment work. In countries where undergraduate education is separated and offered in affiliated colleges, the size of the individual unit is generally reduced. Even the institution as a whole may find it difficult to qualify if a critical number of students on the roll is insisted upon. Many state universities in India and in the Indian sub-continent, have a large number of small colleges affiliated to them which take care of the undergraduate education, while the universities provide only post-graduate and research programmes. The result of this bifurcation is that neither the colleges nor the affiliating universities normally have more than 1,000 to 1,500 students with the exception of a few universities like MS University of Baroda. Few unitary universities may also be exceptions. In the case of a typical institution, for the extent of efforts and the time involved for the assessment work, the outcome may not commensurate with the efforts. It is a futile task to take up a unit that is much smaller than the institution as a whole, *viz.* a university or a college. Table 7 gives data on University X (which is a typical Indian university) that would present a realistic picture.

In one of the workshops on departmental accreditation for science subjects organised by NAAC, the participants recommended that along with the three-stage process of self-study, peer review and final decision by the council, screening for eligibility should be added for departmental accreditation. The criteria for the screening to determine the eligibility of departments for the process of assessment were identified as follows:

Age	: 5 years
Faculty size	: Minimum 6
Courses	: At least 2 programmes (M.Sc. + Ph.D.)
No. of publications	: At least 1 per faculty per year

Table 7: Departmental Profile of University X

S. No.	Department	Programmes	Teachers	Students	Computers	Journals/ Periodicals	Ongoing Projects and outlay	Publications (during last 5 years)
1.	Adult/Continuing Education	MA, Ph.D	2	62	1	5	01 and Rs. 1,00,000	03
2.	Ancient Indian History, Culture and Archaeology	MA, Ph.D	2	19	1	2	02 and Rs. 30,000	--
3.	Biological Science	M.Sc, M.Phil, Ph.D	15	60	4	15	10 and Rs. 24,53,395	104
4.	Chemistry	BJC, MJC, Ph.D	6	75	5	9	07 and Rs. 30,92,000	74
5.	Communication Studies and Research	MA, M.Phil, Ph.D	5	80	2	4	--	--
6.	Economics	MA, M.Phil, Ph.D	5	250	3	10	02 and Rs. 5,15,000	73
7.	English	MA, M.Phil, Ph.D	5	71	1	2	--	64
8.	Hindi and Linguistics	LL.M, LL.B, Ph.D	4	61	2	7	02 and Rs. 30,000	16
9.	History	M.Lib, B.Lib	3	52	1	4	01 and Rs. 75,000	20
10.	Law	Ph.D	11	113	2	4	--	08
11.	Library and Information Science	M.Sc, MCA, M.Phil, Ph.D	1	50	7	4	--	--
12.	Macromolecular Research	MA, M.Phil, Diploma, Ph.D	1	5	3	4	03 and Rs. 65,59,000	16

Table 7: (*Contd.*)

S. No.	*Department*	*Programmes*	*Teachers*	*Students*	*Computers*	*Journals/ Periodicals*	*Ongoing Projects and outlay*	*Publi-cations (during last 5 years)*
13.	Maths and Computer Science	M.Sc, MCA, M.Phil, Ph.D	12	286	31	41	02 and Rs. 13,69,760	51
14.	Philosophy	MA, M.Phil, Diploma, Ph.D	7	103	3	15	02 and Rs. 3,44,000	40
15.	Physical Education	BPEd, MPEd, Ph.D	2	98	2	5	--	06
16.	Physics and Electronics	Ph.D, M.Phil, M.Sc, PG Dip.	10	200	18	10	02 and Rs. 34,23,000	84
17.	Political Science	MA, DPA, Ph.D	4	74	1	4	04 and Rs. 1,70,000	17
18.	Sanskrit, Pali and Prakrit	MA, M.Phil, Ph.D	5	48	2	5	02 and Rs. 30,000	34
19.	Sociology	MA, M.Phil, Ph.D	4	70	1	2	--	08
20.	Tribal Studies	MA, Ph.D	1	16	2	3	01 and Rs. 4,50,000	11
21.	Management	MBA, Ph.D	2	123	20	20	--	02

	in refereed journals
Project	: At least 3 major projects for 6 faculties (> Rs. 10 lakhs each) — Increase in number of projects proportionate to number of faculties
Qualification of teachers	: At least 80 per cent with Ph.D.
Student strength in PG	: Minimum 20 (total)
Research scholars	: At least 1 per faculty

If the criteria for the faculty size alone is applied (minimum 6) to University X, only four science departments clear the eligibility test. Among the four, two departments — the Department of Physics and Electronics and the Department of Mathematics and Computer Science are about to be split into separate departments, leaving only two departments with minimum required faculty. The profile of these two departments is as follows:

Profile	*Biological Science*	*Chemistry*
Year of Establishment	1968	1962
Programmes Offered	M.Sc, M.Phil, Ph.D	M.Sc, M.Phil, Ph.D
Number of Teachers	15	06
Student Strength	60	75
Ongoing Projects and Outlay	10 and Rs. 24,53,395	7 and Rs. 30,92,000
Publications (per year)	21	15

The Department of Biological Science does not clear the criteria on total project outlays and even the Department of Chemistry will be in trouble if the criteria of "minimum Rs. 10 lakhs each for the three major projects" is insisted on. This is the case with the university that has been awarded the institutional grade well above the mid-level grading. The potential of the other universities to benefit from departmental accreditation is more doubtful.

Usefulness to Stakeholders

Another advantage of using the institution as a unit of assessment is its direct usefulness and relevance to the major stakeholders, such as the government that funds, and the prospective students and the employers who hire the graduates. The institution is the unit of funding by the government or the private foundations and trusts all over the world. Though certain specific programmes of studies and many research projects may be funded by different individual sponsors to a faculty or a department of studies, the lasting and sustainable funding — maintenance or block grants — comes only to the institution from the state and not directly to any of the sub-systems. Even the agencies that provide support to individuals insist on institutional commitment for accountability and in many cases the institution is the proper channel through which the transaction takes place.

For entry to undergraduate programmes and in most cases even at the post-graduate level, the students and parents choose an institution for study mainly because of the standing, reputation and the tradition of the institution and not based on the quality of specific academic programme(s). It is the research students who base their choices at the department level. They may benefit more from departmental accreditation but the number of beneficiaries would be insignificant in India. While 88 per cent of the total student enrolments in higher education is at the undergraduate level, 9.5 per cent is in the post-graduate level and the remaining 2.5 per cent is at the diploma and doctoral level programmes. If we take away the enrolment in the diploma courses, the doctoral level students do not even constitute 1 per cent of the total student enrolment in HE. In the year 1998, in general higher education alone the enrolment in undergraduate, post-graduate and doctoral levels was 90.86 per cent, 8.44 per cent and 0.70 per cent respectively. We should note that this is the case of general higher education and enrolment in research is much less in professional areas. To serve that highly specialised small group there are other sources of information and to some extent, even departmental accreditation will not be useful to them. Their choice should depend not only on the standing of the department but also on the specific research facilities available, faculty specialization etc. It is reasonable to expect that at the specialised research level, the students would be enlightened enough to browse through the various sources of information and make an informed choice.

Likewise the public consciousness of academic quality is built around the institution rather than any specific course or degree even though the faculty and the quality programmes contribute to the image of the institution. After all, it is the departments that form the backdrop for the institutional assessment and without them the assessment is impossible. Even the public philanthropy seems to favour the institution as a whole.

There are also certain disadvantages in the choice of the institution as a unit of assessment. An overall assessment-based single grade for the whole institution may not distinguish between the good and bad sub-units. At the surface level, it may appear that even the not so well performing groups are protected under the institutional umbrella. If this is the only reservation against institutional assessment, the reporting can be suitably adapted to include departmental evaluation on specific predetermined aspects. A more realistic and practical difficulty will be in assessing institutions that are large, and offer hundreds of programme options with many thousands of students in one or more campuses and such institutions are very few.

Academic Programmes as Unit of Assessment

The academic programmes as unit of assessment will have the advantage of being well focused and will provide opportunities to look into the micro details. It can provide the right kind of inputs to discriminating beneficiaries like the employer and students. It might not have the difficulties one would encounter in assessing the institution as a whole. However, the disadvantages of choosing this as a unit of assessment are:

- At the national level, the number of such units offering the various programmes will be too large and consequently one would end up with a large number of such units to assess in a 5 or 7-point scale.
- Normally any programme at a given institution may not involve more than a few faculty and a few students and consequently the unit size will be too small for such a big effort.
- Compared to the institution as a whole, the composition and character of the group offering a programme may undergo frequent changes. If a faculty or two move out of the institution, the quality of the offerings will suffer and hence, the outcomes of the assessment may not be tenable for any extended time.
- The programmes of interest to the students and the employers at one time may not be so in a few years. It is likely that some such programmes will not even be thereafter one or two years, thus making the assessment effort futile.
- Even though the programme offerings are done by the department/school, most of the infrastructural facilities such as library, computer centres and other learning resources may be shared with others and their quality is determined by the central governance structure rather than by the departments of studies.
- Many programmes that are inter-disciplinary in nature and offered by more than one department with the varying responsibilities. It may not pose a problem when everything is in order. If there happens to be a bottleneck at any juncture, identifying the cause and taking appropriate value judgments become difficult and this will pose a serious problem in objective assessment.

Faculty/Aspect as the Unit of Assessment

Apparently, the faculty, where related discipline based departments of studies are grouped such as Faculty of Arts,

Science, Languages, Medicine, Engineering etc. constitute a relatively homogenous group with an ideal size to be used as a unit of assessment. Unfortunately such a unit is practically unknown to the stakeholders and therefore may not be useful. It is neither a unit of funding by the public nor a unit of academic offering. Therefore, except for its practical advantage as a manageable sub-unit of the system for assessment, it can offer very little to the stakeholders like the funding agencies, employers or to the students.

An entirely different approach in selecting the unit of assessment will be, to take up the different academic aspects like the teaching and learning process or the research component of either the institution or the department of studies. For example, in England, the HEFCE directly assesses the quality of the research in the departments or schools of studies and rates them for differential funding. This process is done by external peers administered by an in-house unit with well laid out protocols and uses the outcomes to fund the research activities. In Canada, the CEEC has assessed the general education component of all programmes in all higher education institutions of Quebec. In another round of evaluation it assessed the student evaluation policies of all higher education institutions of the province.

To sum up, while the discipline-wise or aspect-wise assessment provides a horizontal review of the select aspect across institutions, the institutional review yields the top down vertical assessment. While the former may be good for well-developed institutions in advanced countries where systems are well in place, the latter would be more appropriate for institutions in the not so advanced nations where putting the systems in place becomes the foremost objective.

5 Implications of Institutional Grades

Functioning on the principles of participation and transparency, NAAC has evolved the accreditation procedures and the accreditation outcome in consultation with the HEIs. What NAAC follows today as its instrument is the collective outcome of national level consultations for eight years, further fine-tuned with the practical experience of eight years. It has also responded positively to the genuine concerns of the HEIs and made two changes in the grading pattern within a period of four years. Any further change may be possible only when NAAC introduces the next cycle of assessment. The rationale behind the current grading pattern and how institutions have to work towards optimising the accepted methodology within this grading pattern are the highlights of this chapter.

In the assessment of NAAC, the grading of accredited institutions has invited quite a lot of discussions about its implications. Some suggest that the UK model of Teaching Quality Assessment, which does not give an overall grade but indicates the attainment on six different aspects on a scale of

1-4, may be followed. Many support the American model that follows the two-point scale of Accredited-Not Accredited status, without knowing the rationale for evolving the Indian model of assessment. In fact, the Action Plan for setting up a National Accreditation Board for Higher Education (NABHE) noted, *"The proposed accreditation system for the country is not expected to be a replica of the systems elsewhere. The accreditation system to be developed for the country is expected to serve certain broad functions which are peculiar to the educational setting of the country."* (Nair, S., 1990) Consequently, the experts involved at the various stages of the development process of the accreditation system have analysed the methodology of the other countries, taken what is best for the present Indian context and have contributed to the current methodology. The outcome is a unique model that perfectly fits into the Indian system appropriate to the purposes it aims to serve.

Brief History of the Grading System

The early attempts to discuss the mechanism to be set up for assessment and accreditation have already been discussed in Chapter 2. The first document that made an explicit mention about the outcome of assessment and accreditation is the Action Plan for NABHE. This document commented on, among the other things, the objectives and functions of accreditation in the Indian context, modalities of accreditation and the rating scale to be used for assessing the institutions of higher education. It noted, *"the new system is expected to perform the following functions:*

(*a*) Conducting periodic assessment and rating of institutions of higher education or units thereof or specified academic programmes which seek accreditation;
(*b*) Granting specified academic status to institutions and programmes on the basis of the assessment;
(*c*) Communicating the results of assessment in a form

appropriate for administrative action, correction and self-improvement; and

(*d*) Evolving broad policy decisions relating to assessment and certification of institutions at the national level, with a view to ensuring higher standards of excellence in different areas of higher education."(Nair, S., 1990)

The document also recommended on grading institutions, with letter grades A, B or C for accreditation and letter grades D and E for non-accredited status which was taken up for discussion by NAAC after its establishment in 1994. The grading pattern with letter grades from A to E was accepted at a national level meeting of the experts in 1996. The cut-off point for the accredited status and the range for each grade were also finalised at the same meeting. This scheme was followed for the first ten institutions that underwent the assessment for accreditation. The institutions had a lot of reservations about the grades B and C. In qualifying terms, if A stands for an excellent institution, B may denote a good institution, and C may stand for an average institution. But the stigma attached to grade B, the symbol of second grade, does not go well with the qualifier of being good in standards. Getting the accredited status itself means that the institution has the threshold level of quality. Over and above that, the system needed levels of accreditation which would convey to institutions that they were doing a good job, but with scope for further improvement. This was the focus of the discussion in the Standing Academic Advisory Committee in 1999, which proposed the grading system with A* (A one star) to A***** (A five stars).

Till 14th March 2002 this star grading was applied with the scale values as given in Table 8.

Under this scheme, the letter A stands for Accredited status and the number of stars denotes where the institution stands in the quality continuum. The institutions that fail to reach the minimal level set for accreditation are not considered for any letter grade in the new scheme. To make the assessment more enabling, the assessment result of the institutions that got less than 55 were not made public.

Table 8: Grades and Scores in the Star Grading

Grade	*Institutional score (Upper limit exclusive)*
A*****	>= 75
A****	70 — 75
A***	65 — 70
A**	60 — 65
A*	55 — 60
Not Accredited	< 55

The grading system of NAAC that used "stars" came under severe criticism on the count that it promoted a 'hotel' culture. NAAC tried to explain that there was no sanctity about the use of the word "star" and the word "level" or a numerical indicator like 1 to 5 could replace it. In other words, Level-1, Level-2, Level-3, Level-4, Level-5 or A-1, A-2, A-3, A-4, A-5 or A1, A2, A3, A4, A5 could have replaced star grading, without upsetting the scale values and frame of reference, and thus maintained the comparability of grades. NAAC continued to putforth its argument but with limited success. There are issues that can be sorted out by a meaningful rationale, but the star issue seemed to be one where no such reasoning could convince the academia. The point that the word "star" could be replaced with other options did not seem to reach many. There was even a dangerous tendency to blame the stars system for any minor roadblock in the progress of NAAC; this caused a lot of concern to the decision-making bodies of NAAC. There was a difference of opinion among the EC members themselves; some strongly felt that there should not be any major change in the grading pattern till NAAC completes the first cycle of assessment at least for the universities, which may hopefully be reached by the end of 2002 or with a few late comers it may go up to mid-2003. The others felt that to avoid further confusion, the star grading should be dropped at the earliest.

To respond to the star debate, that was initiated mostly by the institutions that were yet to get accredited and the academia that were not convinced of the grading system, NAAC decided to modify its grading pattern once again. The Committee on NAAC's Policy and Procedures, constituted by UGC in December 2001 to give recommendations on further changes that might be needed in the NAAC's policies and procedures, also recommended that the usage of star might be replaced. These developments were discussed further by the Executive Committee of NAAC and with effect from 15th March 2002, NAAC follows the nine-point scale that uses a combination of letter grades and pluses given in Chapter 2. With this new grading, the issues of reorienting the stakeholders to the new system of grading, training the assessors appropriately and facing the questions of non-comparable outcomes are being discussed.

The Outcome of NAAC's Process

The outcome of an assessment exercise by NAAC is the recommendation on accreditation and institutional grade. There are three steps in the process:

Criterion-wise judgment: For each of the seven criteria that forms the basis for assessment, the peers look for evidence to validate the claims in the self-study report. To facilitate critical assessment, key aspects have been identified for each criterion. Taking cognisance of the strength of the institution on each of those aspects, the team records the criterion-wise assessment in terms of an appropriate score in percentage.

Application of weightages: Depending on the nature of the unit of assessment, the criteria have been allotted differential weightages. For example, the weightage on research is more for universities than it is for the colleges. Similarly, for autonomous colleges, in view of the freedom they enjoy on curricular design and examination process, the weightage on curricular aspects is more, compared to an affiliated college. The criterion-wise assessment in terms of the percentage score and the weightage attached (given in Table 5) is used to calculate the composite institutional score.

Calculation of overall grade: The institutional score is

converted to an overall grade on a nine-point scale with the scale values given in Table 6.

This revised scheme of grading also causes a lot of concern among the academia.

Concerns on the Multi-Point Grading

Suitability of a grading pattern depends on the purpose it purports to achieve. External quality reviews worldwide have a dual purpose, *viz.* reviews for accountability and for improvement. The emphasis on either one of the two varies between different countries, depending on the degree of accountability required by the various authorities. NAAC's process is focused on the latter purpose — improvement. The objective is therefore to facilitate self-improvement through institutional self-evaluation along with suggestions by an external team for further development. This is achieved well by classifying institutions under a few categories and giving them directions for future development in a detailed report. The top bracket institutions are helped to realise their potential so that they can capitalise on them and maintain their standards. The institutions that fall under the lower brackets are helped to initiate quality enhancement strategies so that they can move towards the next higher grade.

While the above argument is generally agreed upon by the academia, NAAC does face questions like:

(*a*) Why can't NAAC follow the two-point scale of Accredited/Not Accredited status?

(*b*) Why should NAAC follow a multi-point grade and not the ranking?

(*c*) What is the rationale for the validity period of five years for the grade?

(*d*) Within an institution, there are departments of varying performances. How is the single institutional grade justified?

(*e*) Can we follow the UK model of not giving a summative grade?

(*f*) Can we follow the American model of not using grades?
(*g*) What will be the implications of grading on funding?
(*h*) What will be the implications on other academic decisions like conferment of autonomy?

Adopting an appropriate reporting strategy and convincing the academia about its appropriateness are critical to the success of any assessment mechanism and the rationale given by NAAC in support of its reporting strategy is worth reflecting on.

The Two-Point Scale

Some suggest that the outcome should only indicate whether an institution is accredited or not and nothing more than that. This leads to a two-point classification, which is no more than what the affiliating function by the universities could achieve, but perhaps with a higher threshold level. For the complex system of higher education in India that already has substantial built-in checks and balances through the traditional regulatory mechanisms like affiliation, recognition, review and inspection, the simple *Yes or No* as the outcome of assessment is not enough. The traditional regulatory mechanisms are in place to monitor the essential requirement and ensure that the minimal functioning takes place. But the comprehensive assessment and accreditation of NAAC goes beyond the objective of overseeing the minimal performance and enables institutions to become better with relevance and excellence as the frame of reference. This is best achieved by the multi-point grading.

Ranking the Institutions

The two-point scale mentioned above and the ranking suggested by a few others are logically opposite suggestions. The ranking implies placing every institution in a particular position of merit. Ranking the institutions needs a different set of conditions to be fulfilled. First of all it should be possible to cover all the institutions before the order of merit could be finalised. It should be done within a stipulated period of time. As long as it is a voluntary process, it is not possible to assess all the institutions within a time frame.

Even if it is made mandatory to bring all the institutions under the fold of NAAC, ranking the colleges from 1 to 12,600 and universities from 1 to 274 is not meaningful. Institutions are to be evaluated without loosing sight of their distinctive characteristics and their own sets of goals and objectives. Any attempt to compile ranking tables according to some generic criteria is contrary to the principle of institutional improvement, and will be detrimental to the whole quality assurance system. These attempts would be futile since the Indian higher education system is a large and complex system with a lot of diversity. It is difficult to evolve the instrument and methods that can dependably distinguish between institutions of close standing.

It is well known that the attempts by the media groups to rank HEIs on select criteria have received severe criticisms in spite of the research base the media groups tried to establish. Table 9 presents some of the popular ranking efforts.

While the public may look at these rankings as an additional source of opinion, institutional reaction to these rankings has been predictably mixed, with some supporting their use, others opposing it, and most urging caution. The validity of many of these attempts has been questioned by researchers.

Direct ranking, even on the assumption that it could be done with a strong research base in a way acceptable to the researchers, and within a fixed time frame, will put institutions into very fine classification which may make improvement difficult for the institutions at the lower rung. What is required is a middle ground, putting a large number of institutions into a few groupings, which would allow differentiation but preserve a wide range of institutional types with scope for improvement.

Taking cognisance of all these contextual conditions, NAAC has adopted the multi-point grading system where the merit of the institution is given its due place: Institutions are classified

Table 9: Ranking Efforts by Media Groups

Sl. No.	*Country*	*Publisher*	*Outcome*	*Criteria*
1.	UK	The Times	Numerical scores and overall rankings.	Entry grades, student-staff ratio, accommodation, completion rates, firsts, value added, library spending, PG numbers, employment.
2.	Canada	Macleans	Ranking on different clusters of indicators plus overall ranking.	Student body, classes, faculty, finances, library, reputation.
3.	Australia	The Australian Good Universities Guide	Star ranking on different indicators. No overall ranking.	Status and standing, entry, international, teaching and courses, employment, student population.
4.	US	US News — America's Best Colleges	Ranking on six indicators plus overall ranking plus scores on sub-variables.	Academic reputation, student selectivity, faculty resources, financial resources, retention rates, alumni satisfaction.
5.	India	India Today	Ranking one to ten among categories of institutions like arts, science, commerce, engineering, medicine and law.	Academic quality, reputation, curriculum, student care, infrastructure, admission norms, and job placements.

Source: Davis, D., 1996 and *India Today*, 2001.

under one of the nine clusters based on their merit, without loosing sight of the distinct characteristics of every institution. In fact, it is not correct to call it a nine-point scale. It is a two-tier system where at the first level, institutions are classified into two categories — Accredited and Not Accredited. At the second level, only accredited institutions are classified on a nine-point scale.

Accreditation for Varying Periods

Majority of the academia agree that a simple Accredited/Not Accredited status is not effective enough for the Indian context. But instead of grading they suggest that the accredited status may be tied to a certain number of years indicating the level of performance of the institution. In this line of thinking, *Accredited for two years* may imply the need for improvement, whereas *Accredited for five years* may imply a good standing in quality. The supporters of this outcome argue that the indicated number of years achieves the same outcome as grading, but carries with it much less a stigma. But it is the mindset that dictates whether the outcome of assessment is a stigma or not. Even under the accreditation status of varying period, the frame of reference will automatically get reoriented, like equating the *Accredited for three years* to a grade *B*. Whatever negative consequence or adverse effects one could expect out of the star ratings, will be there in the case of varying period of accreditation. An institution with a longer period of accreditation will attract more funds, good teachers, creamy layer of the student population and social repute, like the institutions with a higher grade. In other words, opting for accreditation status of varying period does not really do away with the adverse effects, if any, of the current system of grading.

It is to be noted that the HEIs are not constrained by the validity period of accreditation. After two years of accredited status, if an accredited institution feels that it has made considerable improvements and would like to make a corresponding in its institutional grade, it can always apply for reaccreditation even before the expiry of the accredited status.

Another reason for not adapting variable periods of accreditation is the need for a thorough review of the entire system on some fixed schedule. Following a fixed period of validity of assessment outcome, many countries have already completed one or more cycles of assessment and are in the process of reviewing their methodology for the next cycle. Further, the capacity of the weak institutions to meet the comprehensive assessment very frequently and the purpose it could serve are doubtful.

Scores on a Hundred Point Scale

Giving the exact score on a hundred point scale is another suggestion that is put forward. In any process that involves human factors, however objective they are, there could be some deviation from the exactness or correctness of a score. The combination of self-assessment with peer assessment needs to be viewed with caution. Institutions have the tendency to boost their achievements and underestimate their weakness. It may be the other way also. NAAC has come across quiet a number of good colleges that hesitated to volunteer for assessment since they magnified their weakness and underestimated their potentials. In either case the self-assessment of the institutions needs to be validated. The peers who validate the self-assessment also differ in their ability to rate others. NAAC has evolved suitable pointers for quality, benchmark statements, protocols and procedural safe guards to minimise the subjectivity as well as inter-team and intra-team variances in peer assessment. In spite of all these efforts to ensure objectivity in assessment, one can never claim 100 per cent objectivity. At least in the first cycle of assessment for a complex and diverse system, it is necessary to anticipate a minimal deviation in the exactness of scores and the range of 5 points in the grading system takes care of this deviation.

Variance Within an Institution

Every institution has performing as well as not-performing departments and the overall single institutional grade does not reflect the difference among the departments. While the performers may feel that they deserve a better grade as compared to the institutional grade, the poor performers may play safe in the image of the overall grade. This outcome, at the superficial level, seems to have an adverse effect on the good departments and the Head of the institution cannot use this outcome to point out to the poor performers that they should improve. This is the concern expressed by many administrators, perhaps due to the wrong assumption that the scores of the departments are averaged out.

One should remember that the merit of any mechanism has to be seen in the context of the purpose for which it is evolved and its usefulness. The instrument and methodology of NAAC have been tuned to be holistic and comprehensive towards institutional improvement. The departments will be assessed for the *collective impact* they make on the educational experience of the students and the contribution they make to the standing of the institution. Identifying the weaker departments that need to be strengthened may be done by internal mechanisms by the Head of the institution. The simplest way is to see the annual report of the institution and the self-appraisal of the faculty.

Further, although the focus of NAAC's assessment is not to stamp the departments as good or bad, the achievements of the departments as well as the departments that need to attempt further improvement are given a due mention in appropriate places of the assessment report. Going beyond that limit may not be appropriate for the peer team that is specifically constituted for institutional accreditation. Passing detailed and explicit judgment about the departments would require different kinds of peers and a different instrument and methodology. It cannot be achieved well by a generalist team that goes for institutional accreditation. Since NAAC has a separate instrument and methodology for departmental accreditation, if the institutions expect a more detailed picture of the strengths and weaknesses of their departments, they can always apply for Departmental Accreditation.

The Top Bracket

Institutions and experts have expressed many concerns about the *"what next"* of highly rated institutions, especially if the institutional grade is A or above. Will it lead to complacency? With this thinking, there were occasions when some peer team members worried about awarding the top grade to an institution that was excellent but not a perfect one. In their perception, it is only a close to perfect model, an almost ideal institution that can be placed in the A grade. They also realise that such an ideal system might not exist in India. There is no point in having a top bracket in which none of the existing institutions can find a place. To take care of all these concerns, NAAC's grading system has three subcategories in grade A namely A, A+ and A++. Even for the top bracket institutions, the assessment report of the peer team has a specific focus on 'what next' and the section on *Suggestions for Further Development* enables the institutions to plan further quality enhancement strategies. An institution that has found an entry into A grade with the institutional score of 85 may be helped to maintain its level or reach nineties if it acts upon the suggestions of the peer team. After reaching a higher level of quality, sustaining the same itself needs co-ordinated and conscious efforts and the assessment reports have a focus on facilitating institutions to strive for still higher levels. The suggestion for top bracket institutions may have a developmental approach while the suggestions for the lower level institutions may be towards addressing certain issues of concern.

Why not the UK or American Model?

In UK, the institutions of higher education are subjected to four main forms of external quality assurance processes — Academic Quality Audit, Teaching Quality Assessment, Professional Accreditation of Vocational and Professional Subjects and the Research Assessment Exercise (RAE). While the audit looks at the way institutions manage their responsibilities for the quality of awards offered in their names, professional accreditation is undertaken by a range of professional and statutory bodies. The other assessments are done for purposes of funding. The teaching quality assessment of the subjects, which is mandatory, is based on self-assessment by the institution, and peer review through visits by trained external assessors. The assessors review six aspects of the learning experience and its outcomes: curriculum design and organization; teaching, learning, and assessment; student progression and achievement; student support and guidance; learning resources; and quality management and enhancement. Assessors award grades on a scale of 1-4 for each aspect, where 4 is the highest. In RAE, covering all forms of original investigation to gain knowledge and understanding, the assessments are made by panels of subject experts and researchers of high standing in their disciplines. Each submission for research assessment is given a quality rating, judged against standards of national and international excellence. The outcome is on a seven-point scale from 1 at the bottom through 2, 3b, 3a, 4 and 5, to 5* (five star) at the top. (HEFCE, 1998)

The American model of assessment provides differential "accreditation status" like affirmed, warning and probation. With this status is a type of relationship with the accrediting commission. This relationship is defined by the number and frequency of special reports to and visits by the commission: the more serious the problems of the institution, the more reports and visits until the institution meets accreditation standards or has its accreditation terminated. In other words, in both UK and American models, there are critical elements that make the outcome equal to NAAC's grading system.

Do We Need Another Change?

All along NAAC has functioned on the principles of participation and transparency. It has evolved the accreditation procedures in consultation with HEIs. It has also responded positively to the genuine concerns of the HEIs. It is well known that NAAC has made two changes in the grading pattern within a period of four years, leading to three different grading patterns in the period 1999-2002. Although grading pattern is something that should not be meddled with since it is a critical element that decides about the credibility of the EQA at both national and international levels, NAAC brought in those changes since the HEIs wanted that change. When the first batch of institutions were assessed in 1998 the grading pattern in practice was A, B, C, D, and E which was evolved as an outcome of a national level workshop. Institutions expressed concern over the grade B, which has a stigma, attached to it in the traditional meaning of B grade. The first batch was given only the parameterwise scores without any overall institutional grade and in the year 2000 as a response to institutional concerns it was changed to A* to A*****, once again as an outcome of national level consultations. This change did not lead to any major disadvantage to the first batch, since they were only ten in number and seven of them were in the top bracket. Since the revised system also had the same scale value of "75 and above" for the top bracket, those institutions were given the equivalent in the new pattern. The other three institutions were one level below the top bracket in the old pattern with the scale value of 65-75. However, the revised system had two grades for that scale value — 65 to 70 as A*** and 70-75 as A**** and the conversion to an equivalent grade in the new pattern was a disadvantage to those three institutions, taking them two levels below the top category. They still go with the scores without institutional grade. The next change, which is currently in practice, came in 2002 and so far 46 institutions have been accredited with this new system. As a result today we have institutions of three non-comparable outcomes — first batch with no institutional grade, the next group of around 240 HEIs with the star grading and the new batch of 46 HEIs with the letter grades and pluses.

The grading system of NAAC that used "stars" and had worked well for 240 HEIs had a strong foundation when it was evolved and there are models similar to this elsewhere. The Philippines model uses the classification of level 1, level 2, etc., and the UK model uses the 1 to 4 numerical grades. When these models were discussed at a national consultation, the academia expressed concern about the ambiguity attached to the grading patterns of UK and Philippines. In India, would it make the message clear to the public? Would there be a doubt about which was a better grade—1 or 5? This was an important issue of concern since NAAC wanted to make sure that the outcome would not result in confusing signals. Using stars is not new to the EQA world and the UK model has been using it for the research assessment exercise with the grading pattern of 1, 2, 3a, 3b, 4, 5 and 5*. After weighing the advantages and disadvantages of the different grading patterns, the favoured opinion was the use of a system that is well known to everyone and hence the system of using stars was adopted. However, to respond to the concerns of the academia, NAAC revised it to a nine-point scale.

In the case of the first change in the grading pattern, the non-comparability of grades ended with just three institutions. As their accredited status is coming to an end, soon they would under go reaccreditation and fall in line with others with the new grading pattern. But the change from stars has been a major one. As a result, today, NAAC has a big group on HEIs, around 240 of them, with star rating which is non-comparable to the current pattern of letters and pluses. Such a change cannot be attempted again. The HEIs should realize that whatever is the outcome of this revision, if the credibility of EQA by NAAC has to be upheld, further changes should be done only when NAAC launches the next cycle of assessment. How that should be introduced is yet another major issue to be discussed at the national level which is not attempted in this chapter.

Departure from Tradition

While it is academically sound to insist that the next change in grading should wait for the next cycle of assessment, it is essential that the debate on what is good for the Indian context is kept alive. Whether NAAC can bring different grading patterns for the colleges and universities is an issue that needs a lot of reflection and debate. In spite of the differential weightage to the seven criteria, and contextualisation done by peers, the academia do compare the grades of the parent universities and their affiliated colleges. There have been instances where the parent university got an institutional grade lower than many of its good affiliated colleges. Although NAAC explains to the academia that the grading is not meant to compare apples and pears, comparison of this kind becomes unavoidable and it assumes unhealthy dimensions due to the affiliating functions that bind the parent university and the affiliated colleges together. Instead of differential weightage, opting a different grading pattern itself may be the wayout.

The same agency following different grading patterns for different purposes is not new to the quality assurance scenario. For example, CEEC followed a three-level assessment outcome for Policy Implementation — Policy implementation has satisfactory results, Policy implementation has partially satisfactory results and Policy implementation has unsatisfactory results. (CEEC, 1994a) However, in evaluating the Implementation of the Policy on Evaluating Student Achievement, the Commission used the following four rulings: (1) The policy is entirely satisfactory, (2) The policy is satisfactory, (3) The policy is not very satisfactory and (4) The policy is unsatisfactory. (CEEC, 1994b) Whether a similar strategy would be feasible in the Indian context needs to be explored.

This may be different from our traditional way of evolving a grading pattern. But one should realize that the rapid changes in the environment mean that a quality assurance agency should be maximally flexible, maximally cost-effective and minimally intrusive and flexibility should extend to the adoption of new paradigms. As noted by Woodhouse, external quality assurance is a second order phenomenon, dependent on higher education for its existence and *raison d'etre*. There are issues about the philosophy of, and mechanisms for, quality assurance. Such issues ultimately have no validity in themselves: their validity lies in the extent to which they contribute to the success of higher education. This is true regardless of whether a quality assurance agency is operating as an adviser or as an inspector of the institutions. (Woodhouse, 1998a) In sum, a departure from the traditional way of looking at the grading pattern may be a good option and before NAAC launches the next cycle, these options have to be explored for their advantages and disadvantages.

For sixteen years, from 1986 to 2002, every effort has been taken to evolve an accreditation system that would have the maximum acceptance and credibility in the country. Sixteen years may be a short period for a country like India, which has a long history of providing education through the Gurukula system. But it is long enough a period to go unnoticed when the pressure to provide higher education at an internationally acceptable level is mounting. What NAAC follows today as its instrument is the collective outcome of national level consultations for eight years, further fine-tuned with the practical experience of eight years. Instead of trying to *reinvent the wheel*, working towards optimising the accepted methodology in the current cycle and reflecting on the changes necessary for the next cycle have to come to the forefront.

6 Funding Decisions on Assessment Outcome

In the changing context of the world becoming a global village, imparting higher education of nationally comparable and internationally acceptable 'standards' to a larger population of students has become essential and urgent. This requires quantitative as well as qualitative inputs; quantity in terms of substantial investment and quality in terms of adopting appropriate measures to maximise the outcome with the available resources. Consequently, the governments, which are the major fund providers in many countries, have realised the need to go beyond the fragmentary monitoring mechanisms towards holistic, comprehensive, objective assessment strategies, which will serve the twin purposes of quality assurance and accountability. Consequently, many funding decisions are being based on EQA outcomes and in India the UGC has taken an initiative towards partial funding based on accreditation outcome. This has raised many queries about the implications and this chapter highlights those discussions.

The policy announcement by MHRD and UGC regarding setting a time limit for the universities and colleges to get themselves assessed and accredited by the end of 2002 and the year 2003 respectively has once again brought into focus the relevance and the urgent need for assessment and accreditation of institutions imparting higher education. A similar trend could be seen among more than 100 countries that have established their own national assessment agencies, most of them in the 90s, to take care of the quality concerns of their higher education system. Many of them use the assessment outcome for direct or indirect funding. This is true even in countries where EQA has evolved as a non-governmental initiative.

The United States of America has been following this system for nearly a century. The United Kingdom and a number of European and Commonwealth countries have also established their national accreditation agencies in the early part of 1990s. In India, although NAAC was established in 1994 itself, very much in line with others without the usual time lag. However, there was very limited response from the universities and colleges for accreditation initially, possibly because it is only a voluntary option on the part of the institutions, although there was a tacit understanding that the funding agencies as stakeholders would take the assessment outcome into consideration for funding. On the other hand, the experience in other countries is quite different, but positive.

The International Experience

In the USA, though accreditation is still considered voluntary, several accreditation cycles could be completed largely because the stakeholders give due importance to the accreditation status of the institutions. With six regional accrediting agencies that do institutional accreditation for the HEIs of their jurisdiction, four national accrediting agencies that again do institutional accreditation at the national level and around 60 specialised accreditation agencies, the US system offers an example of how influential the assessment outcomes could be. Today, the State and Federal governments rely heavily on accreditation to spend as much as $60 billion annually in student aid to accredited institutions. Many other federal funds and billions of dollars in state funds are dependent on accredited status. State certification of professionals is heavily dependent on whether or not students have completed accredited programmes. In some professions as many as two-thirds of the states require graduation from an accredited programme for licensure. Other countries rely on the accreditation for verification of quality of institutions and degrees. Decisions by students about where to attend college and determinations by the public about whether an institution is considered "quality" depends on the accredited status. The employers would reimburse the tuition fee to their staff who avail of staff welfare schemes, only if the courses are taken from an accredited institution. All this is happening in spite of accreditation being a "non-governmental voluntary self-regulation". Consequently, even institutions like John Hopkins, Harvard and Stanford universities got themselves assessed and accredited in order to attract students who depend on the student aid fund (fellowships) for pursuing their higher education interests.

The Higher Education Quality Council (HEQC) of the United Kingdom, which has now been replaced by the Quality Assurance Agency (QAA), has already completed one cycle of institutional review and QAA carried out the second cycle of "continuation audit". The QAA since its inception in 1997 has also completed one cycle of programme assessment. This could be achieved because it is mandatory on the part of the Higher Education Funding Council of England, to link its funding with assessment. The HEFCE is legally responsible for ensuring that the quality of education is assessed in the universities and colleges it funds and it distributes public money for teaching and research in universities and colleges based on Teaching Quality Assessment and Research Assessment Exercise (RAE). It has a contract with QAA to conduct Teaching Quality Assessments on its behalf. Assessors award grades on a scale of 1-4 for each of the six aspects, where 4 is the highest. Where any aspect is graded 1, the institution must take action to remedy shortcomings as a condition of future funding. It is true of Oxford, Cambridge and other well-known universities of UK also.

Under RAE, the quality of research is given a rating, judged against standards of national and international excellence on a seven-point scale, from 1 at the bottom through 2, 3b, 3a, 4 and 5, to 5* (five star) at the top. RAE ratings are translated into a funding scale. In 1997-98, for example, departments rated 1 or 2 attract no HEFCE research funds; and a rating of 5* receives four times as much money as a rating of 3b for the same volume of research. The total for all departments in all subject areas is awarded to the institution as a block grant, which it can distribute internally as it chooses.

In Canada, Alberta is the first province to link funding to reward performance in public post-secondary system. Performance is measured in two categories — the Learning Component and the Research Component. The Learning Component had five indicators in three areas — Accessibility, Responsiveness (Graduate Satisfaction, Employment Rate) and Affordability (Administration Expenditures, Enterprise Revenue). The Research Component measured the Research Excellence through four indicators (Council Monetary Award, Citation Impact, Community and Industry Support, Research Enterprise) only for universities. In 1998-99, institutions were awarded $15 million based on their performance. This allocation represented about 2 per cent of total operations grants to institutions. All institutions received a system award, an allocation of 1 per cent of their general operations grant. Twenty institutions were recognised for excellence and received a progress award of either 0.63 per cent or 1.26 per cent. The calculation process was such that the two levels of progress awards would be in a ratio of 2 : 1. That is, the top progress award would always be twice the second level progress award. (AECD, 1995, 1999c)

While the funding envelope of Alberta is a governmental initiative more on the lines of UGC in India, within the same country, the Ontario province offers an example of non-governmental quality appraisal initiatives being used for funding decisions. For the establishment of any new programme it has to pass the appraisal procedure of the Ontario Council on Graduate Studies (OCGS), which is a non-governmental body owned and funded by the 17 autonomous universities of the Ontario province. To continue to have the programme and be eligible for funding from the provincial government, the same rule applies. The Ontario Council on University Affairs (OCUA), an intermediary advisory body to the government on matters related to whether a programme should be funded, considers the OCGS appraisal for its recommendations. It would recommend to the Ministry only the programmes that clear the appraisal of OCGS and the programmes not deemed of "acceptable academic quality" would be excluded from a University's count. (OCGS, 1996)

These are only a few examples to indicate that linking funding with the assessment outcome is prevalent everywhere.

Funding Decisions in India

Even in India, no institution gets grants or subsidies, without assessment in some form or the other. The UGC's development and other special grants under the plan or non-plan funds are sanctioned to the universities and colleges only after the visiting teams visit and assess their performance at the beginning of every plan period. And this has been going on for well over 45 years ever since the UGC was established. The institutions in India have never been hesitant to undergo reviews by the visiting teams and get ready for the review even with a short notice, perhaps because the linkage between such reviews and funding has been always explicit. It is evident from the fact that the entire assessment reviews of all the universities and colleges for the UGC IX Plan development grants were completed in a record time of about four months. When such linkages are not explicit, there is always some reluctance.

International funding agencies for research also look for the accreditation status of an institution even if the project proposals from the individuals or groups are found acceptable.

This will be true for some of the national funding agencies like the Department of Science and Technology (DST), though they have not formally announced yet.

Non-linear Link

There is also a doubt that there will be a linear link between funding and the accreditation status — higher in the rating with more stars more will be the funding and *vice versa*. It should be noted that no such intension has been announced by the UGC so far. However, it should also be understood that the accreditation would have certain implications on the funding. So far the funding agencies have had their own assessment mechanisms for funding based on certain criteria. For some schemes the criteria might relate to the proven achievement and for some others, it might be based on the *social* concern or *locale* of the institution. Whatever is set as criteria, no fund is given without an assessment of how far the predetermined criteria have been/will be fulfilled. Now UGC has implied through this announcement, that it will use the assessment by NAAC for some of its funding schemes that have a direct bearing on quality. For instance, institutions that have demonstrated the potential to provide quality education, though not graded in the high bracket, may be chosen for substantial funding to capitalise on their potential. Those institutions that are rated high need not necessarily get more funds but can be encouraged through appropriate incentives including the recognitions like the designation of "Institution of Excellence", and special status as the "provider of transnational education". Recently, the Tamil Nadu State Government through the State Council for Higher Education has made it a prerequisite to get accreditation for HEIs that wish to apply for either autonomous or deemed university status. Similar moves are on in a few States like Bihar and Karnataka. Only the extreme cases of non-viable units will be watched carefully for their efforts to implement suitable corrective measures without cutting their basic support. A different set of non-linear formula may have to be evolved for each State in the country, based on the current status of higher education in the respective states.

Voluntary *Vs.* Mandatory

One has to realise that UGC and MHRD are only following their mandate of assessment before providing the funds. Fixing a time limit is only to complete the intended exercise effectively. The institutions should not consider it as being imposed but take it as an indication of the interest of UGC and MHRD, in using the external quality assurance mechanism they have established for promoting quality education. Whether the assessment by a national agency is voluntary or mandatory, the outcomes of such assessment processes are meant for the use of various stakeholders like the funding agencies, students, employers and the society as a whole. Similar to an employer who goes to well rated institutions for campus interviews, the government agencies like UGC would like to use the assessment outcomes for a variety of purposes and not necessarily for funding alone.

After all, accreditation by a national agency like NAAC is based on the unified and comprehensive assessment made on certain international format for a broader use unlike some of the existing mechanisms like inspection and fund specific assessments. This general and comprehensive assessment which is valid for up to five years will facilitate the governmental and other agencies in the speedy disbursement of various grants like a single window system, generally thought of in other regulatory sectors without making separate reviews every time.

Further, there are many institutions that draw their support from multiple sources. For example, the State universities are largely dependent on the State Governments for their sustenance and they receive very little from the UGC compared to their budget. The Indian Institutes of Technology (IITs), Indian Institutes of Management (IIMs) and agricultural universities, are not funded at all by the UGC. There are more than 5,000 colleges that do not come under 2-f status and, therefore, are not dependent on UGC for funds besides hundreds of self-financing colleges promoted in recent years. Many of the deemed universities are funded neither by UGC nor by MHRD. There are also a few universities that come under this category.

The vast majority of the institutions of higher education are maintained and funded by the state governments, except for a few central institutions. In many progressive States, nearly 24 per cent of the state budget is spent on education. In states like Tamil Nadu and Karnataka, the state government spending on higher education alone works out to Rs. 600-700 crores per year. Comparing this, the quantum of federal support to higher education will not even be 5 per cent. It is time that the states start raising the question on the worth of the money spent on the system of higher education. One mechanism is to look into the accountability concern and promote quality assessment by using the outcome of assessment for differential and non-linear funding, as discussed above. Performance based development funding is practised world over within the over-all budgetary provisions, taking about 2 to 3 per cent of the total 'Block' grant amount for the development oriented initiatives. Therefore, the state governments and their agencies should now focus on quality enhancement efforts along with the routine traditional funding for the basic needs, without leaving it completely to the central government and its agencies.

In the final analysis, NAAC's process will remain voluntary as it is designed to serve a number of different beneficiaries. If the various funding agencies like to link their support to the process of accreditation, it is only indicative of their interest in getting the best without duplicating the effort. Today the central government (MHRD) and one of their affiliates have expressed their decision to link their support with accreditation.

Dichotomy of the Academia

It is relevant at this point to bring the dichotomous approach adopted by the academic community in this regard. The faculty not only agrees but also welcomes the external assessment by extensive peer review in the realm of their research function. But they are highly resistant for the same if it comes to their teaching at the institutional or programme level. All the research proposals are subjected to intensive peer review before funding and the research papers are reviewed, even internationally, before publication. Virtually all funding for research is allocated selectively, according to quality. The academic community takes the review of their research function for granted and are even proud to have research funds from an agency that rigorously reviews their proposals. They are proud that their research papers are published in prestigious journals, which are known for their rigorous review. But when the question of external review of an institution for the total quality education is raised, they are not only hesitant but tend to resist vehemently.

It should be noted that the quality of educational offerings has declined in the past 50 years or so mainly because of the rapid expansion of the system and the concomitant pressure — both explicit and implicit — to down scale of the standards to facilitate the low achievers. All the other contributory factors for this down slide can be traced back to this single but inevitable pressure. In fact it may not be the making of the academia as there was no other option for them except to respond to the socio-political pressure. However, the need to improve the quality and the standards of provisions up to at least the level of the average achievers, if not the best, has now become imperative. The assessment and accreditation process, which is multi-dimensional, is designed to bring out the strengths and weakness of the system so that effective corrective steps can be taken to reach this expectation. As an external Quality Assurance mechanism, NAAC provides the necessary credibility to the outcome. Therefore, instead of being unduly sensitive and defensive, the academic community should welcome this effort and help in improving the quality. After all, providing the total quality educational experience for the student community is the primary function of the faculty in the universities and colleges unlike the scientists in the national laboratories.

Finally, the process of NAAC is in a sense fully shaped by the HEIs themselves and its their process. Though established and supported by the government, NAAC's entire process of assessment and accreditation is based on the self-study and self-assessment but validated by the senior academicians with long experience. Therefore, it is advantageous to the institutions to get accredited by their own peers whose objective is not to find fault but to be ameliorative. Alternatively, there is the danger of others stepping in to assess the institutions because the stakeholders are not only anxious but demand to know the relative standing of the institutions and the quality of education they provide. Today higher education is no more in its ivory tower and has to cope with the trend akin to the sellers market. Gone are days when the academic community could decide as to what education they should impart. Already the media has found that their assessment and rating of the educational institutions and programmes have been received well by the public and thus are encouraged to review the institutions every year at time of the admissions. International bodies like the International Organisation for Standardisation (ISO) and their affiliates like Quality Council of India (QCI) have expanded their sphere of operation to include education. Quite a few private agencies and corporate bodies are knocking at the doors. Society at large wants to know wherefrom they can get quality education like any other consumer durable and look for a stamp of quality. If the HEIs don't rise up to their expectations and provide the information they want, they will seek and get the same from other sources and it will be a threat to the self-governing nature of the higher education system.

7 Collaborative Assessment with Other Professional Bodies

In India, most of the student population is under the shade of general higher education. The major professional courses absorb nearly 15 per cent. While the University Grants Commission is responsible for coordination, determination and maintenance of standards, and release of grants, professional bodies are responsible for certification of the professional programmes and authorising the candidates to practice their profession. There are more than 30 such bodies of which around 12 are made statutory in India for various considerations. This trend of professional bodies taking care of the recognition of programmes of their respective specialities could be seen world over. The partnership between QAAs and the professional bodies to avoid duplication of efforts is minimal in most of the countries, except perhaps in UK and USA. The developmental stages of the quality assurance bodies in UK and USA indicate that the attempt towards meaningful collaboration with the professional bodies have been successful. India has a good beginning by its collaboration with Distance Education Council (DEC) and National Council of Teacher Education (NCTE). This chapter highlights the efforts made so far and the issues that are yet to be dealt with.

The general higher education caters to around 85 per cent of the total student enrolment. The major professional courses absorb only a small proportion of the student population, that is, 15.1 per cent. In order of enrolment, these are: Law (5.3 per cent), Engineering (4.9 per cent), Medicine (3.4 per cent), Agriculture (1.1 per cent), and Veterinary Science (0.8 per cent). (Desai, 1999) The Indian Higher Education has evolved various checks and balances to tackle the quality concerns of professional courses also. Apart from the review committees, inspections and internal regulatory mechanisms in the UGC-University-Colleges chain, there are many professional bodies that play a significant role in licensing and ensuring quality in disciplines such as medicine, engineering, law, education and agriculture. While UGC is responsible for coordination, determination and maintenance of standards, and release of grants, professional bodies are responsible for certification of the professional programmes and authorizing the candidates to practice their profession. Some of them are authorised to release grants under specific heads and make policy recommendations on funding. There are more than 30 such bodies of which the following are made statutory in India for various considerations:

1. All India Council for Technical Education (AICTE)
2. Bar Council of India (BCI)
3. Central Council of Homeopathy (CCH)
4. Central Council of Indian Medicine (CCIM)
5. Dentist Council of India (DCI)
6. Distance Education Council (DEC)
7. Indian Council for Agriculture Research (ICAR)
8. Indian Nursing Council (INC)
9. Medical Council of India (MCI)
10. National Council for Teacher Education (NCTE)
11. Pharmacy Council of India (PCI)
12. Rehabilitation Council of India (RCI)

These bodies, particularly the statutory ones, are also regulatory in function and therefore look into the minimal requirements. For example AICTE, Medical Council of India, Dental Council and National Council of Teacher Education have the overseeing function to ensure that the institutions have the optimal facilities and potentials to run the programmes satisfactorily. Some of these councils have formed their own "accreditation" boards like National Board of Accreditation (NBA) of AICTE and Accreditation Board (AB) of ICAR. They are the in-house mechanisms established by the concerned councils to serve an internal purpose. They function as a wing of the concerned professional body and serve the specific requirement of the parent body. For example, AB of ICAR does not accredit the private colleges. Thus they fall short of the national stature and also the element of *being external.* It is an exaggeration to say that NAAC is the only national external quality assurance agency in India.

This trend of professional bodies taking care of the recognition of programmes of their respective specialities could be seen world over. In similar systems of education, over and above the speciality councils, there are also comprehensive assessment mechanisms. But the partnership between these agencies to avoid duplication of efforts is minimal in most of the countries, except perhaps in UK and USA. The developmental stages of the quality assurance bodies in UK and USA also indicate that the attempt towards meaningful collaboration with the professional bodies have been successful.

Collaborative Assessment in USA and UK

In USA, institutional accreditation is granted by the regional and national accrediting commissions of schools and colleges, which collectively serve most of the institutions chartered or licensed in the United States and its provisions. These commissions and associations accredit total operating units, *viz.* institutions. Specialised accreditation of professional or occupational schools and programmes is granted by national professional organisations in such fields as business, dentistry, engineering and law. Each of these groups has its distinctive definitions of eligibility, criteria for accreditation, and operating procedures, but all have undertaken accreditation activities primarily to provide quality assurances concerning the educational and training preparation of members of the profession or occupation. Many of the specialised accrediting bodies will consider requests for accreditation reviews only for programmes run by the institutions holding comprehensive accreditation by the national/regional agencies. Some specialised agencies, however, accredit professional programmes at institutions not otherwise accredited. These generally are independent institutions, which offer only the particular specified discipline or course of study in question.

In USA, collaborative evaluation is defined as a cooperative accreditation review process conducted jointly by regional and specialised accrediting agencies at the invitation of an institution. The participating regional and specialised accrediting agencies will identify a single accreditation team composed of representatives from the agencies for the on-site collaborative evaluation. The institution must satisfy each agency's educational standards and requirements in a manner acceptable to the accrediting agency. At the end of a collaborative assessment by a national/regional accrediting body and professional body, there have been instances when two reports were produced — one on accreditation and the other with recommendations to the professional body to serve its purposes. In some visits a single report has been designed to have sections that will serve the purposes of the collaborating partners.

In UK, where quality assessment is tied to funding, collaborative assessment has reached a fruitful stage. For the collaborative assessment in Nursing, the pilot study was first held in December 1997 after a yearlong discussion between Quality Assurance Agency and the concerned speciality council. In Engineering the first set of collaborative assessments was held during 1996-98 and around 30 per cent of the Engineering subjects were assessed in the collaborative arrangement.

With the experience of a few countries, many more are contemplating on adapting such collaborative exercises to suit their systems. All that has to be done is to deliberate on the most effective ways of collaboration that will suit a particular context. An attempt is made in the following pages to discuss NAAC's experience on the collaborative arrangement.

Towards Collaborative Assessment

Even while the concept of NABHE was under discussion the need for collaborative arrangements in India had been felt. The project report on NABHE noted, "Special care has to be taken to include specialists or experts from different professional bodies, on the Evaluation Teams. Where professional organisations (statutory or otherwise) perform the functions of professional recognition or accreditation of programmes, such recognition may be a prerequisite for accreditation by the NABHE. Wherever possible, the assessments by such bodies and the NABHE could be coordinated into one joint exercise." However in the initial stages, the institutions that approached NAAC for assessment were predominantly liberal arts and science institutions and the question of collaborative arrangement did not come to the forefront. As NAAC gained more and more acceptability among the academia, institutions started looking at assessment and accreditation as an enabling mechanism for self-improvement. In addition, there was an overall appreciation for the frame of reference NAAC adopted — quality and not minimal requirement — which made quality institutions volunteer for assessment and the professional institutions also joined this stream.

There is another reason for the professional institutions' interest in NAAC's process. The professional bodies do not have a mechanism for 'institutional accreditation'. For example, if a technical institution has to go for institutional accreditation through its speciality council NBA, every programme of the institution has to be subjected to 'programme accreditation' and even then the programme grades do not lead to a single institutional grade or a single assessment report. This made even the professional institutions to opt for institutional accreditation by NAAC.

In sum, the following aspects promoted NAAC's process

among professional institutions:

(*a*) National and international acceptability of NAAC's process
(*b*) 'Institution' as a whole as the unit of assessment
(*c*) Lack of an equivalent mechanism with the professional bodies
(*d*) Quality as the frame of reference
(*e*) Voluntary nature of the process that added prestige and the stamp of quality to the outcome

The concern expressed by the multi-faculty institutions on duplication of efforts added to this trend. The Indian higher education system is so diverse and complex that in some States the universities have only liberal arts and science departments and oversee the affiliating functions of only the liberal arts and science colleges. In some other states the university itself may have both general education and professional areas of study. Such multi-faculty institutions felt that they had to get ready for too many visits and raised the issue of duplication of efforts. All these factors made the questions on collaborative arrangement more explicit.

Major Efforts of NAAC

In order to ensure the success of collaborative activities, it is important that the concerned bodies identify a mutually acceptable process to review the effectiveness of collaborative evaluations. Being the only national EQA body that has an instrument and methodology for comprehensive assessment, NAAC took the lead to combine its resources and experiences with the specialised knowledge of the professional bodies. At the instance of MHRD, NAAC organised the meeting of various Heads of Professional Councils to deliberate on the need and necessity to

(*i*) Establish functional relationship between professional and accrediting bodies in respect of assessment and accreditation of subjects.

(*ii*) Work on modalities for long-term cooperation and arrive at memorandum of understanding to streamline the efforts of various agencies in a unified direction.

(*iii*) Establish inter-agency linkages to avoid duplication and promote a culture of quality assessment and enhancement.

The first meeting was convened by NAAC and MHRD on November 18, 1996. Participants of the meeting endorsed the following:

(*i*) Accepting NAAC's three-stage process for assessment and accreditation.

(*ii*) NAAC may undertake preparation of self-study manuals for professional subjects in collaboration with respective agencies.

(*iii*) Assessment and accreditation of professional institutions should be a joint endeavour of NAAC and the concerned agency.

It was also agreed that each institution of higher education must be free to decide for itself whether or not to seek accreditation by any particular agency. Based on the discussions, NAAC even went ahead to prepare the draft MoU with the following highlights:

(*i*) NAAC and the professional bodies will, in mutual consultation, select members of the peer team and the chair.

(*ii*) The mutually agreed upon standards shall apply for judging the quality in functioning of the institution and for giving the grades to the institution.

(*iii*) NAAC will be the administrative agency for the process of assessment and accreditation and shall charge fees as approved by its council in consultation with the other agency.

(*iv*) The final accreditation certification to be awarded will be jointly endorsed by both the agencies.

(*v*) The NAAC and the concerned professional body will work out the practical details of cooperation between the agencies and, in general, are to ensure the proper and effective implementation

The second meeting of the Heads of professional bodies was held on 29th September 1997 in UGC and the participants of the meeting agreed that NAAC should go ahead with establishing interaction and dialogue with the authorities of various professional bodies. It was also agreed upon that NAAC could sign MoUs with such professional bodies, which are willing to go about in a collaborative way. So far NAAC's efforts towards collaborative assessment have been successful in the case of two bodies — Distance Education Council and National Council for Teacher Education. However, there has been no request from any specialised institution in other areas for collaborative assessment. But the need emerged when a multi-faculty university evinced interest in collaborative assessment.

Our Experience at a Multi-faculty University

The University had nine faculties of which faculty of medicine, dentistry, nursing, agriculture, engineering and education needed a special approach. For an ideal assessment visit, a formal agreement among the professional bodies and NAAC, would be necessary. But in the earlier attempts, two of the major professional bodies had indicated their reluctance to accept NAAC as the administrative agency for accrediting professional institutions. When a technical university had to be assessed, the concerned professional body was approached for a nominee to join the assessment team, but the professional body wanted the whole exercise to be shifted to them, in spite of not having a mechanism for institutional accreditation. When another professional institution had to be assessed, NAAC wrote to the professional body concerned asking for a nominee and the professional body maintained silence on the issue.

In the absence of a formal mechanism, it was decided

that a modified strategy, which will incorporate all the critical elements of collaborative assessment, should be attempted. It was also noted that such a strategy should help NAAC to instil confidence among the professional and multi-faculty institutions and also give indications to the professional bodies about how formal agreements can flow from that experience without sacrificing the objectives of both the partners.

In the actual collaborative assessment, the format of self-study report, criteria for assessment and the key aspects to be assessed are to be worked out jointly by the collaborating partners. NAAC did the same exercise with the specialists who have served in the various inspection committees of the professional bodies and evolved detailed guidelines for the data to be submitted by the professional departments of study. Again, instead of the professional bodies nominating their experts, NAAC identified experts who would be accepted as peers in the specialisation concerned and included them in the team as Subject Specialists.

For the first time, the concept of subject specialists was experimented. The protocol and the role of the subject specialists were made clear to the team members. Normally a team of 3-5 members visits an institution and the team stays together and visits all the units together for 3-4 days and finalises its recommendation on accreditation. But in the case of subject specialists they were invited to visit only their areas of specialisation and to give the recommendation to the core group. In this experiment, along with the core group of four members there were 9 subject specialists for the faculty of medicine and nursing, agriculture, education and engineering. In the five-day visit, the subject specialists spent the first two days on the evaluation of the specialised faculties. When the specialists went to their respective faculties one-core group member joined each of those teams. After spending a day in the respective faculties, the specialists gave their inputs to the core group.

The format of reporting to be followed by the specialists was also made in detail to assist the core group in its final decision-making. The evaluation was in terms of department-wise score in percentage, evaluative remarks, justification of the score in the NAAC's Frame of Reference, overall score for the faculty of study and assessment report under the seven criteria of NAAC. The core group used this later when the overall assessment of the institution had to be made.

As an outcome of this experience, the following critical elements were identified for further discussion:

- Interface between the requirements of the agencies that enter into collaborative assessment,
- Clarity on the role of the assessors representing the collaborating agencies,
- Reporting the outcome, and
- Financial implications to the different parties involved.

Although the issue of financial implication did not arise in the modified strategy, the other concerns came up during the team discussion and while arriving at a consensus on value judgment. On the whole, it was a successful experiment and revealed that if there is a demand from multi-faculty institutions for collaborative assessment, entering into formal agreements with other professional bodies would be feasible. In future, as more and more multi-faculty universities are to be assessed for institutional accreditation, institutions may insist that the assessment visit by different professional bodies and NAAC may be coordinated to conduct an evaluation process that would require one self-study report, one on-site visit by one evaluation team, and produce one coordinated evaluation report. In fact, before embarking on the next cycle of assessment the collaborative approach will have to be firmed up and this will become a major agenda.

The Options

In the early stages of implementing, the process of collaborative review develops most efficiently with two collaborating accrediting partners like NAAC and NCTE. The outcome informs the participating agencies and the public of significant strengths and weaknesses of an institution and its programmes. However, in the case of multi-faculty institutions, collaboration of more than two agencies is necessary. One of the following two models of collaborative assessment may be suitable:

Model 1*: The professional body may suspend its own inspection visit, wherever appropriate (certainly not in all cases) and use the assessment report of NAAC for its decision-making.*

This calls for a lot of discussions among the agencies involved to ensure compatibility between their expectations and the actual outcome. The state governments have already based their decisions on the outcome of accreditation. For example, for recommending the affiliated colleges for conferment of autonomy, the State Government of Tamil Nadu has decided to use the assessment report of NAAC. But it does not rule out the separate inspection team's visit for autonomy. It only insists accreditation above a mid-level grading as a pre-requisite for autonomy. If the government of Tamil Nadu, any state for that matter, collaborates with NAAC, collaborative visit will be more fruitful. The implication is that when the assessment team visits the affiliated college, it may have a nominee from the concerned state and care will be taken to see the potential of the college with reference to the criteria and guidelines given by UGC for conferment of autonomy. In fact autonomous colleges rated high by NAAC have expressed that the review committee's visit for review of autonomy may be replaced by accreditation outcome itself. In the long run, methodical efforts may have to be taken to replace similar mechanisms of the professional bodies by the comprehensive assessment of NAAC.

Model 2*: A single assessment team including the representatives of the Professional Body may carryout the assessment in one visit with the common instrument and methodology.*

This joined or integrated assessment becomes useful for institutional accreditation of professional institutions. This requires a perfect understanding between the agencies involved of their roles and responsibilities and the protocols. In consultation with the professional body the instrument may be modified without any violent deviation. To maintain consistency in NAAC's frame of reference, the basic guidelines and the methodology should remain the same. This is being attempted in the assessment of Distance Education Units and Teacher Education Units in collaboration with the Distance Education Council of Indira Gandhi National Open University and NCTE respectively. NAAC had a series of workshops to evolve the guidelines for the assessment of distance education units and the draft guidelines have been prepared in consultation with DEC. In fact, an official of DEC was with NAAC for a few months to workout the instrument and methodology. After a series of consultative meetings, NAAC and NCTE have signed the MoA to assess all the teacher education units of the country.

The judgment on the best model depends on the need of the collaborating partner and the type of institution. Model 1 is suitable to replace the regulatory functions and the concerned professional bodies may suspend their visits for that academic year at least, taking into consideration the report of the assessment team by NAAC. Accordingly the methodology can be worked out. How long can a professional body suspend its inspection and for what purposes can it be done are questions to be discussed. The period of validity of NAAC's outcome is five years whereas some of the inspections of the professional bodies are annual and some are for specific purposes like "granting approval for starting a new course". Depending on the purpose of inspection, an agreement has to be reached on the relationship between "level of accreditation and period of validity of the certification for a specific purpose of the professional body".

As mentioned earlier, Model 2 would be more appropriate for professional institutions where the role of the subject specialists becomes important. As of now, NAAC constitutes assessment teams inviting specialists known for their contribution in the field of specialisation of the institutions.

The assessment of distance education units and teacher education units is expected to be the trend-setter for second option.

Future Perspectives

The experience with DEC and NCTE is expected to throw light on further fine-tuning the following aspects for collaboration with other councils:

- — Protocols and guidelines for collaborative visits
- — Role of the professional bodies personnel in the assessment team
- — Criteria for assessment and procedures to suit the different agencies involved
- — Reporting the outcome
- — The follow-up after the collaborative assessment
- — Financial implication to NAAC, the institution and the professional bodies involved

NAAC is contemplating on initiating the next level of dialogue with the professional bodies. The initiatives with DEC and NCTE may clear the apprehensions of the other professional bodies and bring out the intricacies involved in such collaborations.

Part III: Practices and Prospects

With the strong foundation given by the policy framework, NAAC progressed to implement its procedures towards maximising the acceptance among academia. Although the policies are well laid down, the system had to face unique problems due to contextual factors and the response from the system of higher education was mixed. Suitable strategies were evolved to overcome the problems, to suit the contextual conditions. Through well-planned strategies, NAAC progressed from the stage marked by 'mistrust, rejection, hesitation and apprehension' to the stage of 'appreciation' by the majority of academia. This Part focuses on these developments. It also highlights the future perspectives of quality assurance agencies working together and NAAC's role in the same.

8 Institutional Response

No one questions the importance of monitoring student progress and using the information collected to assist the students who are not performing to their potential. It is equally important to measure the performance of the institutions of education. But when NAAC promoted the concept of performance evaluation of HEIs, there was some reservation on accepting the concept. An important aspect for the success of performance evaluation of institutions is to ensure the acceptability and accuracy of the outcomes. As NAAC worked towards ensuring the acceptance of the academia and fine-tuned the methodology, more stakeholders started basing their decisions on accreditation outcome. Today NAAC has reached a stage of working for large volume of assessment and exploring the other dimensions of quality assurance. This chapter highlights these developments.

The response from the system to the comprehensive-national-external-quality assurance agencies has been mixed the world over. In India, it can be seen in three phases. Phase I was the initial stage of NAAC where strategies to convince the system and getting acceptability by the majority was the focus. Phase

II was the crucial period of operationalising the accepted methodology and fine-tuning the same. Phase III is the current period where some of the stakeholders have given a clear indication that the outcome of assessment and accreditation will have a major role in their decision-making. This has put a pressure on institutions of higher education to undergo assessment and accreditation leading to large number of them approaching NAAC.

Phase I: First Three Years of Striving for Acceptability

Academia knows only too well that anything that is imposed on the system will be rejected. If quality assessment has to lead to self-improvement and if it has to remain as an enabling and ameliorative mechanism, the only way to achieve success is by convincing the system on the merits and allowing the institutions to take their own time to get ready for assessment and accreditation. Therefore, it was decided that in the initial years assessment and accreditation would be voluntary.

This conscious decision was also based on the fact that in the London Model of higher education prevalent in the country, there are adequate checks and balances built in to ensure accountability of institutions; NAAC's process need not be made mandatory to address the accountability issues. Moreover, India has to go a long way to ensure access and equity to a larger percentage of the population and an overemphasis on accountability may become counter-productive. In spite of the huge network of higher education only 6 per cent of the relevant age group are enrolled in higher education.

In the first phase of three years, the institutions were either indifferent or reluctant to volunteer for assessment and accreditation. Some of the reservations they had on external assessment were the following:

(*a*) The checks that already exist in our system like the various review mechanisms of UGC and University and hence whether NAAC's efforts will lead to duplication of efforts,

(*b*) The implications of lower rating,
(*c*) Adverse effects it could have on the institutions and students,
(*d*) Relevance in the affiliating structure, and
(*e*) Suitability of the model to Indian soil since it was wrongly perceived to be borrowed American model.

Major Efforts of NAAC Towards Acceptability

NAAC had to apply a multi-prong approach to clear the apprehensions discussed above. Care was taken to ensure that its strategies had the following elements:

(*a*) The assurance to stakeholders about its independent autonomous stature and commitment to quality assessment,
(*b*) Advisory committees for consultations on academic decisions,
(*c*) Broad involvement and consensus building to ensure widespread support in evolving the norms,
(*d*) Careful development of methods and instruments for assessment and accreditation,
(*e*) Rigorous implementation of procedures, and
(*f*) Transparency in all its policies and practices.

Seminars and academic interactions were organised with various groups of academia at the national level, familiarising them with the concept of assessment and accreditation. A wide range of promotional material was prepared and distributed to thousands of teachers of higher education. The materials include three booklets — *Assessment and Accreditation: How to go about...*, *Frequently Asked Questions and Answers*, and *Relevance of Assessment and Accreditation in the Indian Context*, which would answer most of the queries and apprehensions of the academia. The *NAAC News* — the quarterly newsletter of NAAC also added to the efforts to reach out to more number of institutions. Further, more than 100 awareness activities were conducted throughout the country involving the various universities,

Colleges, State Councils of Higher Education, State Governments, Directorates of Collegiate Education and other forums like the All India Association of Christian Higher Education and the Association of the College Principals.

Through a series of consultative interactions with a large body of academia NAAC evolved the norms, methods and a series of instruments for assessment and accreditation. Among the norms, it was decided that NAAC may concentrate on institutions as the unit of assessment, with provision for assessing individual departments, and that accreditation should continue to be a voluntary process and the outcome will be valid for a period up to five years. The methodology for the process of assessment and accreditation was fine-tuned through a series of interactions and workshops. Detailed manuals and guidelines were published to cater to the different segments of the Indian Higher Education system.

NAAC also had active interaction with other quality assurance councils in India and brought the major national professional bodies of India to discuss and to evolve a method for collaborative assessment. International linkages were established with USA, UK, Canada, South Africa, France, Mauritius and many other countries, for sharing the information and experience. In fact, the training strategy for the National Cadre of Assessors who would visit institutions on behalf of NAAC for quality assessment was evolved in collaboration with the Higher Education Funding Council of England and the Quality Assurance Agency of UK. With the participation of the British experts, training programmes were initiated and today the national cadre of trained assessors has around 200 experts on roll, which will be strengthened further by similar programmes. For the first two training programmes a UK expert was a part of the resource team after which NAAC has become self-reliant in the training strategy.

Teleconferences, bi-national conferences, joint research and publication programmes, academic exchange programmes, participation in international events and study visits to other quality assurance agencies were used to broaden the horizon of NAAC's perspectives. As an active full member of

INQAAHE, NAAC organised the 6th bi-annual conference of INQAAHE in India during March 2001.

All the above-mentioned strategies helped NAAC to cross the stage of trying to convince the system of higher education about the merits of EQA, which ushered in the next phase of operationalising the process.

Phase II: The Next Two Years — Period of Operationalising the Strategy

One hundred and eighteen institutions of higher education — ten universities and 108 colleges, underwent the process of Assessment and Accreditation during this period. For a vast system of higher education, this is a small number — less than one per cent of the total number of institutions. But in terms of the efforts that have gone in for fourteen years in evolving an acceptable methodology of EQA for such a complex system and the field experience of five years, there is enough data to reflect on.

The experiences and institutional response of this phase should be seen in the light of the purpose of the task. For any quality assessment, there can be one or more of the following four purposes. The most commonly stated purpose of quality assessment is accountability by providing assurance for worth of the money to the fund-giving agency. The next purpose is self-improvement of the institutions of higher education. The third purpose is to provide comparative information to a much wider group of stakeholders to enable them to make choices and decisions. The fourth purpose is to stimulate competitiveness between institutions and departments by linking assessment to rewards and incentives.

In NAAC's process of assessment and accreditation, the first and foremost purpose is self-improvement of the institution, which is promoted by the preparation of the self-study report and strengthened by peer assessment; other intentions become the second order consequences. For example, UGC's decision to make accreditation mandatory for all the universities is a major step to use the outcome of assessment and accreditation for purpose of accountability. Facilitating an informed choice by students and parents is served by the web site of NAAC, which presents the profiles of the accredited institutions and the full quality assessment report of the institutions. The public disclosure of institutional grades has already created a healthy competition among the institutions. In all these purposes, whatever is the extent of realisation of the purpose, the way institutions have responded during and after assessment and accreditation was found to have a wealth of information, which was useful to fine-tune the methodology. The significant impact institutional accreditation had on institutions during Phase II is highlighted in the following pages.

Impact of AA on the Institutions

- NAAC's process has made institutions realise that institutions alone are responsible for their quality matters.
- Institutions initiated discussions on their specific goals and objectives and the means to achieve them.
- The greatest effect of undergoing the process has been on innovative programmes taken up by the institutions beyond the mandatory requirements of the affiliating system.
- An increase in the programme options could be observed.
- The autonomous institutions that had the freedom to innovate in curriculum and the affiliated colleges that were offering a few programmes of their own restructured the curriculum.
- The attention of the institutions became focused on the right priorities and responsibilities especially with reference to teaching and learning as their primary mission.
- It has stimulated a research culture, which is more pronounced in colleges that were focusing only on teaching.
- Most thought that it was a promising tool for

improvement of their documentation especially on teacher appraisal, student progression, alumni profile and placement services.

- It focused the attention of the institutions on to the support services within their reach, which they never thought of.
- Although information technology was entering into all institutions NAAC's process made its need felt by all sections of the institutions instead of confining the benefits to a few sections.
- Training the staff on new communication technologies, faculty development programmes, and student activities gained a new dimension. They were seen as useful investment on human resource development of the institution.
- Small differences were forgotten and the faculty and management became united.
- Departments that were functioning like islands within the bigger system started sharing their experiences and expertise.
- It also resulted in healthy competition among the departments each unit trying to maximise its contribution and achievement.
- Alumni involvement and parent involvement in improving the institution became explicit.
- Things taken for granted were rediscovered like their unique characteristics and strengths.
- Quality Assessment triggered new healthy practices. Informal mechanisms like student feedback on teaching were institutionalised.
- Institutions realised the importance of projecting their strengths and unique features to the society to get good resources — funds, students and teachers.
- Community oriented activities, extending expertise to the development of the immediate neighbourhood, initiating research that would solve the problems of the neighbourhood, students and faculty participation in those activities etc. increased.

- The management perception on issues like faculty work load, pay scale of the management paid staff, role of the management in supporting the research culture, encouraging faculty and staff development, inter-personal relationship between management and the other units of the institution, role of those units in the management decision making etc. changed towards participative, open and transparent style of management.
- Focus on future plans became clear and vision and mission documents and perspective plans were drawn up.
- They realised that the process of institutional accreditation had done much more to revive and stimulate the quality culture of the institution.

Overall Appreciation for the Process

Although the overall response for assessment and accreditation has been positive, as a consequence of the diversity and complexity of the large network of higher education system, the extent of appreciation for the process was different in each institution. The response of the sub-units of the institutions like the departments can also be characterised as positive and optimistic. Institutions of all categories, starting from the ones that were placed at the lowest rung of the classification to the ones that are placed at the top bracket, have uniformly claimed that the assessment and accreditation made a significant change in their pedagogical, managerial, administrative and related aspects of functioning.

However, the extent of appreciation differed depending on the following:

(*a*) Correlation between the expected grades and the actual grade.
(*b*) Autonomous *versus* Affiliated nature of the institutions.
(*c*) First batch *versus* later ones.
(*d*) Institutions that are yet to undergo the process.

The institutions that have received a lower grade have recorded many critical comments about the various aspects of the process including the criteria, format for self-study, peer team composition and reporting the outcome.

There was also a difference between the institutions that had experienced autonomy and institutions that were in the affiliating structure, in their appreciation for the process. This divide could be seen at the stage of volunteering for the process itself. While 32 per cent of the autonomous colleges, nearly one-third (44 out of 138), have undergone assessment and accreditation, which is a very significant percentage, only 1.44 per cent of the affiliated colleges, 182 out of 12,600), have undergone assessment. Many affiliates were of the stereotypic thinking that the parent-university is responsible for every malady. Some complained that the assessment process is not sensitive to the constraints of the affiliating system.

The next major divide in the response of the institutions could be seen between the first batch of institutions that underwent the process with the earlier grading scheme and the others who came in later. The first batch was not given the overall institutional grade; they were given only the parameter-wise scores. When the later ones got the institutional grades, it led to non-comparability in the outcomes leading to many unhappy notes from the first batch. The Academic Council of NAAC is to consider this issue and take a decision on whether the first batch too may be given the overall grade.

The abovementioned factors have greatly influenced the perception of the institutions on aspects like reporting the outcome, duration of the visit, nature of visit and many other issues. Today NAAC faces a different set of questions mostly on the process and outcome. Some of them are given below:

(*a*) Is the advice given by the NAAC peer teams qualitatively relevant?

(*b*) Is the motivation for self-improvement produced by the process on the faculty sustainable enough?

(*c*) Is the accreditation cost justifiable when the funding agencies like the government and the UGC are steadily withdrawing their subsidies? Will it not be better if the institutions spend the accreditation cost on campus development?

(*d*) Why should NAAC call its process voluntary while UGC is trying to make it mandatory?

(*e*) Why does NAAC leave the parent university and the government in assessing affiliated colleges, while the government pays 95 per cent to 100 per cent of the expenses and the parent university has a lot to contribute to the quality of its affiliates?

(*f*) Why should the outcome of NAAC lead to the prospect of grading, if the objective is only to give ameliorative guidance for self-improvement?

(*g*) Does NAAC look upon politics and trade unions as blots upon the campus?

(*h*) How does NAAC ensure its accountability? Who will assess NAAC? Why can't NAAC give the academic community an opportunity to evaluate the process of assessment and accreditation even as it conducts its evaluation in individual colleges?

(*i*) Why should NAAC assess an institution as a whole, which will give a single grade not differentiating between good and bad departments?

(*j*) Why can't NAAC do programme assessment which will be useful to students?

(*k*) What are the benchmarks and indicators NAAC has evolved for placing the institutions under various categories?

To clear the apprehensions listed above and arrive at a consensus on issues that needed to be debated, NAAC initiated rigorous academic exercises during Phase II. For many such discussions, the lessons learnt during the institutional visits and the feedback from the assessors formed the base.

Major Efforts of NAAC in Phase II

The issues that arise out of the above mentioned questions

and the response of the institutions discussed earlier were analysed and identified for further action. The issues were found to cluster around the following:

(*a*) Unit of assessment
(*b*) Benchmarks and performance indicators
(*c*) Objectivity of peer assessment
(*d*) Reporting the outcome
(*e*) Evaluating the evaluation

Taking cognizance of the genuine concern raised by the academia, NAAC developed procedural safeguards and protocols that have already proved their positive impact on fine-tuning quality assessment. Efforts of NAAC on each one of these issues is given below.

Unit of Assessment

It is important that the unit of assessment is chosen keeping in mind the national context. During the first three years of academic consultations and discussions with a large number of academia, NAAC found that the opinion on Institution *versus* Programme accreditation varied a lot. By then NAAC had its Academic Advisory Committee to advise on academic decisions and the issues that were considered to have a bearing on the unit of assessment were taken up for discussion and some of them are as follows:

(*a*) Size of the national system of higher education,
(*b*) Specific purpose for which the assessment has been commissioned,
(*c*) Significance of the outcomes to the stakeholders,
(*d*) Viability of assessment in terms of having a minimal critical size for assessment, and
(*e*) Feasibility of completing the assessment within a pre-set assessment cycle

Due to the various considerations listed above, the Academic Advisory Committee recommended to NAAC decided that it should promote the institutional assessment in the first cycle with provision for departmental assessment, which was then approved by the Executive Committee of NAAC. These considerations have been discussed in detail in Chapter 4 of this book.

Benchmarks and Performance Indicators

Benchmarking is measuring performance against that of the best-in-class organisation, determining how the best in class achieves those performance levels, and using the information as basis for goals, strategies and implementation. To facilitate this process, NAAC has identified seven criteria, which encompass every aspect of functioning of the institutions of higher education. Further, for each criterion, key aspects and criterion statements have been identified and defined, and they serve as benchmarks. In addition, the pointers of quality for each one of the key aspects of the criteria to facilitate the peer assessment were developed at this stage.

Objectivity of Peer Assessment

Having accepted peer assessment as an integral part of the methodology, NAAC has taken note of the factors that result in variances within a team and between teams and conscious efforts have been made to minimise the same. The protocols and procedural safeguards were fine-tuned during this phase to make peer assessment as objective as possible. Apart from the safeguards, a sub-committee reviews the peer team reports and the recommendations of the sub-committee are placed before the Executive Council of NAAC. The senior academicians of the EC, who share the common agenda of promoting quality assurance in higher education, look into every aspect of the visit and the peer team report and after a thorough analysis of the same, take a decision about the accreditation status of the institution. This ensures that the peer teams assess institutions from NAAC's perspective without varying greatly in their frame of reference.

Reporting the Outcome

This is an issue of contention world over. To serve the primary stakeholder — institutions that undergo the process — and the other major stakeholders NAAC has adopted the pattern of disclosing the overall grade and the detailed evaluation report. Discussions are still on towards making it better.

Evaluating the Evaluation

This process of meta evaluation was done during this phase. Feedback was collected from institutional heads and assessors on their experience and perception on NAAC's process. The outcome of this analysis formed the basis for the fine-tuning of NAAC's process on many aspects.

With the shift in institutional response from resistance to acceptability, some issues on fine-tuning the process have been sorted out and some issues are still under discussion. As the fine-tuning continues, there has been an increase in the number of institutions that volunteer for assessment. This has resulted in Phase III with associated challenges of a new order.

Phase III: Taking it Forward

Ensuring that the governments take the assessment outcome seriously for their decisions is one such strategic role to take assessment forward. NAAC has succeeded in roping in the support of the important bodies at the centre as well as the states. UGC's decision to link the development grant with accreditation status is evidence to this fact. The enthusiasm of some of the state governments also needs a mention. The DCE of the Tamil Nadu government has made the accredited status with mid-level grade and above as a prerequisite for colleges that wish to apply for the autonomous status and deemed university status. Karnataka has made accreditation mandatory for all professional colleges. Similar moves are on in states like Bihar, Kerala, Goa, Andhra Pradesh and Maharashtra.

State level Coordination Committees have been constituted for overseeing the process of accreditation. NAAC has promoted its partnership with the states by developing action plans for them to meet the UGC deadline of 2003 to get the colleges accredited. In Karnataka and Maharashtra efforts of NAAC have already resulted in drafting a comprehensive action plan for the states. Similar discussions are on in other states also. The action plan includes an analysis of the assessment reports to identify the strengths and weaknesses of the institutions in the state and suggesting ways to remedy the weaknesses. The areas of concerns facing the weak and less privileged institutions will be addressed with specific recommendations to UGC, State Governments and MHRD as the next stage, for need-based funding. There are also proposals to provide some more schemes and support for quality enhancement. Institution of Internal Quality Assurance Cells, and visit to high quality institutions for familiarising with the good academic practices will also be encouraged. It is heartening to note that many decision makers and policy makers take NAAC's efforts seriously and the increasing involvement of the state governments is becoming more pronounced.

The initiatives mentioned above have made institutions realise the trend that more and more stakeholder decisions will be based on assessment outcome in future. However, a more organised relationship between accreditation, policy decisions of the governments and the decisions of the other funding agencies, mainly for quality enhancement schemes is yet to emerge. There is a consensus that in a developing country like India that has a long way to go in increasing access to higher education, linking accreditation with basic funding may not be appropriate. But the expectations of the institutions on incentives for maintaining higher levels of quality and support for further quality enhancement cannot be ignored. While UGC's decision on development grants is a positive step, till recently, the major providers — the state governments—were yet to take note of the assessment outcome of NAAC in a significant way except in one or two states.

As these stakeholders make their choices clear, more and more institutions will join the main stream of quality assessment. NAAC also realises that the stakeholder decisions can only stimulate the quality culture but it is the responsibility of the institutions to sustain the same. In other words, institutional participation in quality assessment and commitment to sustenance of quality has to become an integral part of the functioning of the institutions. All these developments have led to more challenging issues and some of them are listed below:

(*a*) Managing large volume of assessment,
(*b*) Minimising inter-team variance in large volume of assessment,
(*c*) Follow-up and documentation of outcome of assessment,
(*d*) Institutional expectations on incentives and disincentives for the level of accreditation,
(*e*) Focus of the next cycle of assessment,
(*f*) Preparing the institutions for the next cycle,
(*g*) Recommendations to MHRD/UGC for policy decisions,
(*h*) Making the institutions take more responsibility for their quality,
(*i*) Collaborative assessment with speciality councils, and
(*j*) The international agenda on mutual recognition of outcome of accreditation.

To address the emerging issues of Phase III, NAAC has chalked out a future plan and plan of action, which are under discussion.

(*a*) NAAC anticipates to assess and accredit institutions in large number in unit time. This has resulted in the need to develop suitable co-ordinating mechanism to handle high volume assessment, *e.g.*, assessing about 20 institutions per month on an average. A plan of action has been evolved for the same.

(*b*) NAAC has a successful collaborative assessment strategy with two agencies — National Council for Teacher Education and Distance Education Council. The methodology and instruments have been developed and implementation will be taken up soon.

(*c*) NAAC will focus on continuous improvement of the instruments developed so far with the help of the advisory committees and through interactions with the other international councils

(*d*) The National Panel of Assessors will be expanded through further training.

(*e*) NAAC has the mandate to make recommendations to UGC/MHRD that will facilitate their policy decisions. Therefore, analysing the region-wise assessment reports to give recommendations to MHRD and UGC has been taken up and the outcome will have to be finalised.

(*f*) Standardisation and development of quality indicators in line with the international trend and exchange of information with other countries on quality assurance activities will be taken up.

(*g*) Extending mutual recognition through MoU (with other countries) for credit transfer and mobility of students by assuring the quality.

(*h*) Developing and pooling of quality assurance expertise at the national and regional levels of the world.

The mid-term review with the assessors and institutional heads — people who have seen the process from both the sides of the table — has thrown more light on the mid-term correction necessary in the plans of NAAC, especially on issues like assuring the academia the objectivity of peer assessment, providing guidelines to sustain quality, place of quantification in quality assessment and the larger role NAAC has to play in projecting the quality institutions at the international level.

9 Ensuring Objectivity in Assessment

Assessment is a human process and people differ markedly in their ability to assess. This difference gets further accentuated in the Indian system of higher education, which is large, complex and diverse. In spite of wide experience, the diversity in the Indian higher education system leads to significant difference in the background and experience among the members of the assessment team and accordingly ones understanding and appreciation of an institution varies. Depending on the team composition, the interplay of these factors in the team leads to inter-team variances and that is a serious threat to the objectivity of assessment. NAAC has taken note of the influences that result in variances within a team and between teams and conscious efforts have been taken to minimise the same. This chapter highlights those safeguards and protocols.

While the institutions that have experienced NAAC's process are appreciative of the objectivity in assessment, there are many institutions that have a major hesitation on this issue. When NAAC officers interact with institutions that are in the pre-assessment stage, they come across a lot of queries, which hover around the ones given below:

(*a*) How *Reliable* is the process? If the institution is re-assessed by another team, will the outcome be the same?

(*b*) How *Valid* is the outcome of assessment? How truthful is the assessment in serving the purpose for which it has been initiated? If the purpose of assessment is to measure the quality of education, does the outcome reflect it truthfully?

(*c*) How *Objective* is the process? Is the assessment free from the personal bias and prejudice of the people who are involved in the process? What are the safeguards to eliminate or minimise the influence of personal baggage and equations?

Some of these doubts may be due to the genuine concern of the institutions. After every academic activity, the NAAC team discusses the outcome and feedback received from the experienced peers, to ascertain what more could be done to fine-tune the methodology and instrument. During the discussions NAAC has always been clear that the intention is not merely to find out ways and means of convincing the institutions but to analyse how best the genuine concerns expressed by the institutions could be honoured without compromising on the objectives of NAAC. Such discussions have always led to new initiatives to make NAAC's process more systematic and data based. This chapter is an attempt to share the measures that have been taken up by NAAC to make assessment as reliable, valid and objective as possible.

Factors that Influence Assessment

There are two issues that need to be taken care of. First of all, the objective of the process as well as the methodology for the same has to be clear. Once that frame of reference becomes acceptable, the operationalisation of the instrument and methodology has to be done systematically and rigorously to maintain objectivity throughout the implementation of the mechanism. The first issue deals with clarity in the policies and procedures, which has evolved over a period of fifteen years beginning from the discussion on the Programme of Action to translate the New Education Policy-1986. To implement the recommendations of this document, the Accreditation Committee was constituted to work out the modalities for the Indian context and the recommendations of the committee have been deliberated in a series of national level workshops. The outcome is the methodology that is followed today. In other words, there is clarity in the policies and procedures of NAAC.

Most issues of the second type — operationalising the mechanism, boil down to the question of objectivity in peer assessment. In fact peer assessment is an integral part of any system and the academia have no hesitation to accept its indispensability in research funding, selection of personnel and many examination oriented procedures. Peer Assessment is one of the critical elements, similar to self-studies that have evolved as internationally accepted components of external quality assurance. The significance of peer review in quality assessment, though still under debate, has not found a better alternative, in any of the quality assurance agencies. For specific agenda like linking a part of funding to certain management statistics of the institutions and financial support according to student number mechanisms have been worked out without peer review. But for quality assessment, the role of the peers becomes indispensable. Having accepted peer assessment as an integral part of the methodology, what can be done to get the best from it?

Peer Assessment

One should be aware that assessment is a human process and *People differ markedly in their ability to rate/assess.* In any assessment process, one may come across three kinds of people. Some are generous and their assessment outcome is always an

Above Average status. They can indicate the difference between the best and the worst only in terms of *over and above the mid-point of the rating scale.* For anything less than a perfect score, they try to be doubly sure of concrete evidence for having to pull the score down and invariably the benefit of doubt is given to the assessee. There are some at the other extreme. They start from a minimum score. They have strong opinions about how an assessment should be done, what should be the outcome, how to differentiate between the *good* and *not so good* etc. They carry a lot of *personal baggage.* The third category constitutes the majority. They may not be sure of their frame of reference and play cat on the wall. They go by the decisions taken by the others in the group. This gets further accentuated by the difference in the background of the members of the assessment team. In spite of wide experience, the diversity in the Indian higher education system leads to significant difference in the background and experience among the members of the assessment team and accordingly ones understanding and appreciation of an institution varies. Depending on the team composition, the interplay of these factors in the team leads to inter-team variances and that is a serious threat to the objectivity of assessment.

NAAC has taken note of the influences that result in variances within a team and between teams and conscious efforts have been taken to minimise the same. NAAC's assessment as a data based and systematic method has been achieved through concerted efforts at three levels — at the preparatory stage, during the peer team visit to the institution and finally, at the decision making level by the Executive Committee (EC) of NAAC. The efforts that are put in at every stage are given below:

At the Preparatory Stage

Clarity of purpose: The purpose of assessment and accreditation and how it is different from that of the inspectorial committees has been discussed in many consultations and seminars. There is a clear understanding among the academia that NAAC's process is a holistic and transparent process of trying to understand the institution and identify its strengths as well as areas that need further improvement. It is neither an exercise of fault-finding nor is it judgmental in nature. It is seen as a voluntary effort of the institution to share its self-analysis with a team of equals, with the purpose of further improvement.

Clearly spelt criteria: As mentioned earlier, the series of national level discussions gave a broad outline on which assessment could be developed. These broad areas have been further fine-tuned resulting in the seven criteria which form the basis for assessment. Any significant aspect of functioning of an institution of higher education gets covered under one of the seven criteria, leading to a holistic picture of the institution under assessment.

Key aspects identified by NAAC: Under each criterion aspects of importance have been spelt out. This gives a direction to the peer team to look for excellence in the most relevant aspects. The very fact that every aspect of functioning of an institution is given a due place is an evidence to promote convergence towards systematic assessment, and thus it ensures focus on the purposes of assessment.

Guidelines to institution: To facilitate the process of preparation of the self-study report NAAC has developed manuals and guidelines that give operational suggestions on the process. The framework for data collection given in the manual enables institutions to understand the kind of data expected for assessment. It also helps the institutions to organise the data in a meaningful way. With the clarity on expectations, the three Ws become clear — What, Why and How? The outcome is a document that presents a true picture of the institution, which is essential for a reliable assessment.

Choice and training of peers: While maintaining consistency in assisting the institutions, NAAC brings in consistency among the peers by appropriate training and discussion strategies. This greatly reduces the inter-team variance that may arise due to difference in the frame of reference. The discussion and training are also meant to eliminate the personal bias of the peers and give them the NAAC perspective. They come to realise that they have to act on behalf of NAAC during institutional visits and this promotes objectivity in their assessment.

Handbook for assessors: This again is an attempt to spell out clearly the roles and responsibilities of the members of the peer team, make explicit, in concrete terms, the purpose of every session and provide hints to the peers to facilitate their interaction with the various constituents of the institution.

Maintaining link between different teams: In addition to the training and discussions, the inter-team variance is greatly minimised by maintaining link between different teams. Though institutional comparison is not the purpose of assessment and accreditation, it becomes an unavoidable consequence of grading the institutions. The peers who have seen and experienced similar institutions for accreditation, have a great role in maintaining the link between teams.

Appropriate composition of the peer team: Normally, to constitute a four-member team, a panel of 15 to 20 members is suggested to the institution and out of this the final team is constituted. While finalising the team composition, various aspects like the strengths of the institution, its unique characteristics, location, organisational structure, size etc. are taken care of. Though it is not possible to have an expert for every programme and area of functioning, care is taken to have a team that will understand the institution from all its significant perspectives. Recently, for one of the panels, NAAC had to go through the database of hundreds of experts in a particular area of science to identify the right expert, since the institution to be visited was strong on that specific area.

Consultation with the institution: Since the whole process is a transparent one, where the focus is self-study and the institutional efforts have to be presented truthfully, there is no secrecy at any part of the process including the decision on visit dates and peer team composition. The visit is planned during mutually convenient days and the institution is consulted for the panel of experts who could be considered for constituting the final team. If the institution has reservation against any member, it may be brought to the notice of NAAC without suggesting any alternative. Though NAAC takes care of the choice of peers, to the best of its knowledge, some micro but important details may not surface initially and consulting the institutions at such times has been found to be useful. In one of the panels there was an expert — who was awarded an honorary degree by the institution to be visited and it was brought to the notice of the NAAC staff by the institution. When the institution brings such details to the notice of NAAC, leaving those members for possible conflict of interest, from among the others the final team of 3 to 5 members is constituted.

No conflict of interest: Once the choice of the peers is made, NAAC finds out whether the peers have any conflict of interest with the institution to be assessed. Though the peers are experts known for their integrity, to ensure and assure objectivity, the peers have to sign the *no conflict of interest statement.* It makes sure that the peer does not belong to the same State where the institution is located and that the peer has no affiliation with an institution competing directly with the institution to be assessed. It also requires a certification that the peer has no involvement with the proposed institution, directly or indirectly through any close relatives, in the past or at present, as either an employee or a member of any official body, or a consultant or even a graduate. This method of getting the certification on no conflict of interest has been of practical help. One of the panels had a member whose spouse was working in the institution to be visited and the expert himself brought it to the notice of the NAAC staff. In another instance the peer's son was a student of the institution. Such members do not find a place in the final team. The institution signs a similar statement also. It also requires a certification that none of the members of the proposed team will be appointed at least for a year for any important assignment in the institution.

In-house analysis of self-study report: The self-study report submitted by the institution is analysed by the in-house personnel of NAAC and any information gap or discrepancy in data is taken care of by the NAAC team. This enables the projection of a holistic and true picture of the institution as far as possible. Though the peers would validate the institutional inputs during the institutional visit, the first impression about the institution influences the peers' tentative evaluation and NAAC takes care of presenting the data in an objective way.

Peer team document preparation: The in-house NAAC team prepares a *peer team document*, which has been designed to bring inconsistency in the way the peers would take value judgment. Starting from tentative evaluation to final grade, it helps the peers in recording the reasons for the value judgment, issues to be probed further and evidence required.

Pre-visit analysis by peers: This being an exercise on mutual trust, the peers trust the information provided by the institution, and try to relate it to where it can be placed in the quality continuum. The pre-visit preparation requires the peer to record the tentative assessment of the institution, with reasons for the tentative score. That brings focus to the peer assessment and prepares the peer to look for information gaps as well. The pre-visit analysis slowly frees the peer from any preconceived notion and opens the way to an open-minded analysis.

Pre-visit briefing and team discussion: Before the actual visit to the institution, the peer team has a briefing by the Chair of the peer team and the NAAC team and the team discussion that follows normally irons out individual differences. When the members begin the actual visit at the institution, they function as a team on behalf of NAAC with clarity on their roles and responsibilities.

During the Visit to the Institution

During the visit the peer team visits all the facilities and departments, scrutinises relevant documents and interacts with various constituents of the institution — representative group of students, parents and alumni. For every interaction, the agenda is clearly spelt out in the peer team document, which almost becomes a work-book for the peer team. The peers record extensive notes in their documents. Here again, in line with the policy of transparency, whenever the team agrees on an issue of concern, it is shared with the concerned authority or the head of the institution and the feedback is obtained. In fact, an important session towards the fag end of the visit is a *discussion with the Head of the institution on the outstanding issues.* This is followed by another session wherein the draft report itself has to be given to the institution. If the institution has any observation on any aspect of the report, may be omission of some data or factual error is detected, it is then discussed with the peers. In addition, the visit has at least three peer team discussions, in which the members discuss among themselves, the highlights of their assessment and check for the evidence for the same.

In a nutshell, during the visit to the institution the following aspects help to bring in objectivity:

(*a*) Sequencing of visit schedule with ample scope for visiting facilities, interaction with the various constituents of the institution and review of documentary evidence
(*b*) Clear agenda for every session
(*c*) Peer team discussions placed at various stages of the visit
(*d*) Sharing of issues of concerns among the team members
(*e*) Looking for evidence especially for any hard remark about the institution
(*f*) Frame of reference given in the peer team document to record value judgment on the strengths and weaknesses of the institution
(*g*) Focused report writing
(*h*) Checking correlation between scores and the report
(*i*) Finalising the report at the venue itself
(*j*) Emphasis on transparency in the process
(*k*) Sharing the report with the head of the Institution

After the Visit

After the visit, the peer team reports are scrutinised by a sub-committee and the recommendations of the sub-committee are placed before the Executive Council of NAAC. The senior academics of the EC, who share the common agenda of promoting quality assurance in higher education, look into every aspect of the visit and the peer team report and after a thorough analysis of the same, take a decision about the accreditation status of the institution. This ensures that the peer teams assess institutions from NAAC's perspective without varying greatly in their frame of reference.

Although these efforts have been found to be fruitful in minimising the inter-team variances, a lot more can be done further and NAAC is contemplating the following:

(*a*) Orientation for the co-ordinators of the steering committees (institutional facilitators) who co-ordinate the preparation of the self-study report.
(*b*) Conference for the peers to share their experiences.
(*c*) Strengthening the dialogue between NAAC and the peers and keeping them updated through NAAC bulletins.
(*d*) Maintaining consistency in the composition of the peer teams for a homogenous group of institutions.

The procedural safeguards and the protocols developed by NAAC have already proved their positive impact on ensuring the objectivity of quality assessment. As NAAC builds on its experience and the experience of the other quality assurance agencies, these strategies are sure to further strengthen the process.

10 Performance Indicators in Quality Assessment

In more than 100 countries where some form of accreditation is in practice, the accrediting agencies base their evaluation on a set of predetermined criteria or standards. The peer judgment with reference to the predetermined standards becomes the indicator of quality. In an effort to make this evaluation as objective as possible, various approaches are being considered. Performance Indicator (PI) has occupied a major part of those discussions at many levels and a debate on its place in the quality assessment exercise in the Indian context is necessary. This chapter highlights the role PI could play in quality assessment in Indian context and NAAC's efforts to balance peer assessment with quantitative indicators.

The term performance indicator is used in many ways by different interest groups. A definition suggested by Cuenin (1987) says that performance indicators are "measurement for assessing the quantitative performance of a system". If one has to analyse the institution as a system in totality, PI can be identified with reference to input, process and output. *Input Indicators* are concerned with the resources and factors employed in order to produce an institution's output. *Process Indicators* relate to the way in which resources and factors are combined and used in order to produce the institution's output. *Output Indicators* describe the outputs of the institution. These indicators are certainly useful to see *whether the inputs have been transformed to outputs of expected standards through appropriate processes.*

The Performance Indicators may be grouped in many ways. The Jarratt Report (1985) of UK proposed three kinds of Performance Indicators:

(*a*) Internal Performance Indicators,
(*b*) External Performance Indicators, and
(*c*) Operational Performance Indicators.

Internal Performance Indicators include the following:

(*a*) Market share of undergraduate applications (by subject),
(*b*) Graduation rates and classes of degrees,
(*c*) Attraction of masters and doctoral students,
(*d*) Success rate of higher degrees (and time taken),
(*e*) Attraction of research funds, and
(*f*) Teaching quality.

External Performance Indicators include the following:

(*a*) Acceptability of graduates (postgraduates) in employment,
(*b*) First destination of graduates (post-graduates),
(*c*) Reputation judged by external reviews,
(*d*) Publications by staff and citations,
(*e*) Patents, inventions, consultancies,
(*f*) Membership, prizes, medals of learned societies, and
(*g*) Papers at conferences.

Operational Performance Indicators include the following:

(*a*) Unit costs,

(*b*) Staff/student ratio,
(*c*) Class sizes,
(*d*) Course options available,
(*e*) Staff workloads,
(*f*) Library stock availability, and
(*g*) Computing availability.

Source: Jarratt 1985:53.

Kells (1992) recognises two types of indicators, namely those used by government and by institutions. *Indicators for government* include nationally defined measures of institutional responses to government goals and policies (equality of access, reservations). *Indicators for institutions* include institutional management indicators (workload, student enrolment, financial trends) and teaching, research and service indicators (examination results, publication and citation analysis, finished product quality). In keeping with this classification, in the United Kingdom, a distinction is made *between Macro-performance* indicators that are indicators of the higher education system as a whole, and *Institution performance indicators* that may be applied to individual institutions.

In the Indian context, studies have focused on a few broad areas like Mission Oriented Indicators related to Teaching-Larning, Teaching Performance, Research Performance and Financial Performance. The manpower related and student related input and output indicators have also been researched into. The following indicators give a glimpse of the focus on Input and Output related indicators.

Input Related indicators are as follows:

(*a*) *Physical Resources:* Availability, Utilisation, Concern for efficient and economical use of physical resources.
(*b*) *Manpower Resources:* Teaching and research hours, Supplementary efforts by teachers, Vacancies filled, Student coverage in terms of SC-ST-OBC and gender.
(*c*) *Financial Resources:* Use of budgetary instruments, Index of mobilization of resources, Built-in flexibility in

resources availability, Concern for economy and efficiency, Autonomy in the use of resources.

(*d*) *Democratic and interactive ethos in the Institution:* Index of involvement of the concerned parties, Autonomy in decision-making, Autonomy in implementation of decisions.

Output Related indicators are as follows:

(*a*) *Immediate:* Results of student evaluation and teacher evaluation of the process, Results of final exam of students.

(*b*) *Extended:* Performance of students and teachers in their future career.

Studies have also classified indicators into micro-, macro- and mega-indicators. *Micro-indicators* are those that relate to specific operations within a sub-system that have a bearing on overall performance. An example is the method of identification of courses and programmes in the process of learning materials development. *Macro-indicators* include those areas of performance that are of aggregate nature like entry-exit performance of students. *Mega-indicators* are those areas of performance in which an open university, as a special sub-system, interacts with the social system as a whole. Examples are the ratio of formal education programme to non-formal educational packages, and the nature and extent of the institute's interface with industry.

A cursory look at the above indicators will convince any one that they are useful for institutional improvement. On every aspect given above, an institution can always fix its target at the next higher level of performance and work towards it. But the impact of PI may go beyond the institutional context to reach the external audience — the beneficiaries.

Expectation of the Beneficiaries

PI may be used by the institution to inform the beneficiaries about the extent to which their expectations may be fulfilled by the institution. In its simplest form, the PI may be used to present the institutional profile to the public, as a marketing or image building strategy. The beneficiary, depending on the specific purpose and expectations, will do the value judgment. For this purpose, regular publication of PI, as done in many developed countries, on what the institutions can offer and at what cost, will have to be promoted. In fact this has been done by some of the media groups, though not in a systematic and scientific way and it has received a lot of public attention. If done objectively, PI will present the profile of the institution in a limited perspective to different audiences — government, student, public, industry, funding agencies.

The purposes served for some of the external interest groups are given below:

- *Student:* Choice of institution
- *Parent:* Worth for money
- *Government:* Accountability, funding, policy and planning
- *Funding Agency:* Funding research and development
- *Society:* Accountability
- *Industry:* Institution-industry linkage, funding, graduate employment (Davis, D., 1996)

If PI is to be used as a means to serve institutional improvement and marketing, it is a welcome aspect as an *internal management strategy*. Once its application goes beyond the institutional context and aims at value judgments, the issues of concern arise regarding the appropriate usage.

PI in Value Judgments

There are a few bodies in the country like UGC, NAAC, AICTE, NBA, MCI etc. that take up value judgments of institutions or programmes. Though these bodies vary greatly in terms of their agenda for the value judgment, their frame of reference, the outcome and the implications, they can broadly be put together in two categories.

Category I:

Agenda: Granting of recognition or affiliation to institution/programme.

Frame of Reference: Ensuring satisfactory conditions to achieve the stated objectives of the institution/programme.

Outcome and Implications: If conditions are met satisfactorily, recognition is granted. Otherwise, the institution/programme cannot continue.

Category II:

Agenda: Assess and Accredit institutions/programmes.

Frame of reference: Standing of the institution/programme in the quality continuum.

Outcome: Grade denoting the quality of the institution/programme.

Implications: Low grade does not lead to the discontinuance of the programme or closing of the institution. Public disclosure of the grade will build societal pressure. Students, teachers, funding agencies and government may use the grade as an indicator to make decisions on choice of the institution for various purposes.

Under the value judgment of the first category, satisfying the minimum requirements becomes important. The use of quantitative, standardised set of indicators that can cut across a group of similar institutions is useful in this context and they will truly indicate whether the institution/programme has the threshold level to deliver what it purports to, in a satisfactory manner. For example, it is meaningful to say that an institution should have a minimum campus area and infrastructure, library stock, student-teacher ratio, qualified teachers, adequate working days, ...to provide satisfactory educational experiences. Here the focus is on the input factors based on the assumption that adequate inputs, when combined with monitored and proven processes will lead to satisfactory outputs. The difficulty arises when the use of PI is extended directly to fit it into the quality framework.

Under value judgment of the second category, quality becomes the focus and not quantity. It is true that minimum requirements are needed to achieve quality. But, the indicators used for ensuring minimum requirements cannot be applied as such for the value judgment of quality. In the Indian context, institutions that volunteer for assessment and accreditation are the ones that are confident of their potential and it is common sense that they have already crossed the stage of *struggle for survival*. An analysis of these minimum requirements with reference to the institutions that have volunteered for Assessment and Accreditation indicates that all of them are placed at a comfortable position.

Further, take any indicator that is used in category I; more of quantitative aspect does not necessarily lead to better quality. This clearly indicates that one has to limit the use of the PIs used by the category I agencies to the screening level where the eligibility to enter into assessment and accreditation may be determined. It is even reasonable to say that the norms of the indicators of category I may be pitched slightly at a higher level for the screening for quality assessment. Once institutions/programmes cross that critical level for the quality assessment, the shift should be towards 'processes' focusing on how the inputs are optimally used to maximise the outputs.

Quality Assessment: Shift in the Focus

When there is a shift in the focus of evaluation, there should be a corresponding shift in the indicators and the PI that is being used with reference to minimum requirement are not sensitive enough to reflect this vital variance. Therefore it becomes essential to think of a different set of PI, the ones that may not be related to the minimum requirements, but have a bearing on quality. For further discussion, the PI related to Teaching and Research Output is considered.

For any institution of higher education, the major output may be derived in terms of teaching, research and consultancy activities. It is difficult to quantify the teaching and research output of an institution with reference to the quality framework. The first difficulty comes at the stage of deciding the balance between teaching and research — how much of teaching and how much of research, one can expect in any institution. Institutions vary a great deal in the importance they give to these two dimensions. How much of research can one expect in a Teaching-oriented institution and how much of teaching can one expect in a research-oriented institution? It is obvious that the institutions do not just fall under the two categories of teaching-oriented and research-oriented institutions. Each institution is unique with reference to the teaching-research mix alone. Without an answer to this question, how to judge whether the output is up to the expected level or not?

Then comes the next difficulty. Take the case of an institution that has been focusing on both teaching and research. Can the number of graduates and post-graduates produced by the system measure the teaching output? Can employment rate indicate the quality of teaching? Can the cost of education be linked to it? How to estimate the expected research output of the institution in quantitative terms? In terms of the number of papers, projects, consultancy, inventions and patents, awards and recognition, and Ph.D. programmes? Even if it is attempted, how to take cognizance of the quality of the output?

Research Output

In all the aspects mentioned above, as possible indicators of research output, if numbers are given importance, large departments and established departments will be at an advantageous position and the new ones though with good potential may be at a disadvantage. In an effort to bring in the quality dimension, if elements like giving weightage to the type of the journal, length of the publication etc. are considered, it will only make things more complicated. It should also be remembered that publication is not the only way to disseminate the research finding. Seminars, group discussions and informal peer interactions are as effective as publications for which performance indicators will not be sensitive.

Citation index has similar drawbacks.

Research income, if taken as an output indicator, will put some institutions at a disadvantaged position. Research grant is scarce in some areas of study and an institution that focuses on those areas may attract very little research grant. Moreover, good research need not always be costly. Some subjects need expensive inputs for research and they get more research grant while some rely more on human resource. If this issue is not noted well, the outcome will be that the institutions will project higher expenditure for their research proposals. What could be achieved with fewer resources will end up as an expensive experiment.

Teaching Output

The number of graduates and post-graduates as an indicator of teaching output may be analysed by the dropout rate and pass percentage. The accepted terminology now is "Non-completion rate and Success rate". Whatever is the term used, it depends on the difficulty level of the subject. Further, during the first year of the undergraduation, drop out rate is high in science courses due to entry into professional courses. In some courses that are taken for stopgap arrangement, the non-completion ratio is very high. This happens more at the post-graduate level and students at this level drop out mainly due to gainful employment. Sex, entry qualification and locale of the institution are other factors that influence the non-completion rate. Female students, low entry-level achievement of students and rural locale of the institution are the factors that put an institution in a disadvantaged position.

Employment rate also depends on the nature of the subject (vocational or academic) and the avenues for further studies available in that subject. The sex and socio-economic status of the students also play a crucial role. All this only implies that the abovementioned aspects, to be used as PI, need to be adjusted, corresponding to a variety of factors related to the nature of the institution. Any kind of oversight in this will result in misleading indications.

Other Issues

If the PI is not sensitive to the distinctive characteristics of the institutions, a greater danger will be seen after a few years. When institutions become very conscious of the PI, they will seek to maximise performance on the same set of indicators. This may result in institutions competing with each other, by mere duplication or imitation of the efforts of the other institutions, with the sole agenda of moving towards a higher rung in the PI rating. Consequently, the diversity among the institutions of higher education might be lost.

Another concern that questions the use of PI in value judgment of quality is about the ways in which it will influence the quality. Institutions may try to improve only on the aspects that take them to an advantageous position with fewer efforts. There will be a tendency to make up for a weakness in a major area by improving the performance in another area, which will merely adjust the indicators. That is, the institutions may emphasis on certain aspects of performance at the expense of some of the major ones. This itself may lead to deterioration in quality.

Peer Judgment Guided by PI

This chapter does not argue that the higher education sector should not attempt to quantitatively measure its quality. It is true that there can be little hope of progress towards developing appropriate methods of evaluation unless satisfactory measures of quality can be constructed. In fact, the higher education sector has no alternative but to develop such measures. But the point to be taken seriously is that PI may be useful as a management statistics but for purposes of quality assessment it is inadequate and needs to be balanced with other data.

What NAAC has attempted on this issue is worth mentioning here. On receiving the self-study report from the institution, the academic group of NAAC works on it and prepares an *in-house analysis document*. This document presents the statistics NAAC has arrived at by analysing the data from a sample of "good" institutions. The guidelines given in the document suggest that the institutional aspects need to be looked into, giving due credit to the standing of the institution on these aspects, in the light of the statistics provided. Whenever the institutional context demands that a particular statistics is not relevant, the peers record the justification and go by their judgment. A brief outline of NAAC's experience with the quantification efforts is given below:

Indian Experience with Credit Points

In NAAC's process institutions are assessed under seven criteria and for everyone of those criteria, key aspects have been identified. For example, the key aspects identified for the criterion on Curricular Aspects are given below:

Criterion I: Curricular Aspects

- Compatibility of the programmes with goals and objectives
- Initiation, review and redesign of programmes
- Feedback on programmes
- Interaction with academic peers and employers
- Programme options

A need was felt to develop pointers for each one of the abovementioned key aspects to facilitate the peer assessment. For a particular aspect, if the existing situation in most of the good institutions were marked, by pitching it a little higher it would be possible to fix a higher level of classification. Similarly, lowering it a little will give another category. Based on this thinking, NAAC collected data from a representative sample of around 40 good institutions and averages were calculated. For some aspects it was possible to fix a three-level classification and in other places a two-point scale was fixed. After a thorough discussion with a group of experts, it was piloted on a few institutions.

Where to Draw the Line?

The pilot study has indicated a few valuable lessons. During the pilot study, the peers were given guidelines which required them to give due consideration to the *credit points* evolved by NAAC while taking value judgment based on the criterion. The teams have expressed the usefulness of these credits as a point of reference. The concern expressed by some of the experts that whether the credits will become misleading was found to be baseless since the peers always applied their judgment and moderated the use of the credits. The teams also took care that they did not take judgment on discrete aspects. For initial focus on aspects of importance the credits were taken as the referral point. But when it came to the judgment of the team on a criterion, the outcomes on individual indicators needed to be synthesised and the peer assessment became vital there. For example, the student-library book ratio was very favourable in one of the institutions that had many years of history. It had long working hours, open access system and book bank facility. If the team goes by those aspects alone, for library facilities, the institution should come under the top bracket. But a closer scrutiny revealed that over the years the institution had accumulated books but the quality of the books, currency, money spent on it, implementation of the book bank facility, support services of the library, linkage with other libraries, and maintenance were not satisfactory. As one can see, for some of them the quantification in terms of a ratio may indicate the level to which it may be assigned to and for the others it has to be a qualitative judgment in terms of good or satisfactory or poor. The peers had to synthesise both qualitative and quantitative inferences and arrive at a holistic value judgment.

Another example is the Computer Centre as a learning resource. Norms have been evolved for the number of computers available in the centre, working hours, output of the centre in terms of computer assisted learning packages, software available and maintenance of the centre. An institution may be in the top bracket with reference to the number of computers and software available. But the working hours of the computer centre, policy of the institution to use the centre to support student learning, access to teachers and students, support staff available, financial implications to the students etc. may not be very encouraging. Only the peer team can take all this into cognizance and take a holistic judgment.

Contextualising the indicator was also found to be working effectively in the teams. To cite an example, last year NAAC visited a college run by missionaries, which was offering a lot of consultancy service without charging the beneficiaries. The peers took a judgment about the quality of consultancy offered by the institution and recorded that the output of the institution was commendable. Though the institution has not earned a single rupee out of its consultancy activities, the peer judgment gave the right context to the evaluation. Examples can be cited for most of the statistics on financial aid to students, employment rate, curricular options, infrastructure, learning resources and placement services, to substantiate how the peer judgment became crucial in contextualising the assessment. To put it in a nutshell, NAAC saw that the peers had an important role in moderating the credits, synthesising the outcome on individual indicators and contextualise the same. The mere use of indicators would have been misleading.

NAAC makes a careful choice of the peers who are well known for their wide experience in higher education, contribution to their field of knowledge and respected for their integrity. In spite of the emphasis on experience and expertise, the difference in their set of mind leads to not only inter-team variance but also to intra-team variance. The differences in the perceptions get minimised when they analyse the institution's standing with reference to the credit points. However, teams have expressed their concern about the danger in using the credits when some of them attempted to allot credits for various aspects and then converted the credits accrued to criterion-wise score in percentage.

The experience with credit points has given the conviction

that quality assessment in a complex system cannot be dictated by PI. While quality assessment itself is a new culture that is slowly being nurtured in the system, over emphasis on PI will defeat the very purpose of Assessment and Accreditation. Then where to draw the line? Allowing variance for the institutional differences, PI can be used for inter-institutional comparison on areas such as how much could be spent on a particular head, what could be the employment rate one could expect etc. and that too for purposes of internal management and improvement. In the quality assessment, PI may be used at the screening level and anything more than that, such as rating on teaching output, research income, student progression etc. should be balanced with peer judgment.

In an effort to be more objective one should not forget the precautions to be taken in using indicators in measuring quality. Even as one of the many input, how PI can facilitate or mislead value judgment becomes another aspect to be debated. The quantitative inputs on which the PI heavily relies upon need to be judiciously balanced with the qualitative inputs and that is exactly the process followed by the accrediting agencies world over. Especially in the case of quality assessment by accrediting bodies like NAAC where the methodology is already a blend of peer judgment guided by relevant statistics, there is no immediate need to overemphasise the role of PI.

11 Institutions Rated High by NAAC

What Makes them Different?

The educational system has always been the subject of constant change however slow the change process might be. As institutions established by the society, educational institutions are affected by changes in society and at an ideological level, all educational institutions implement change. While some institutions implement changes successfully and reach the desired outcome, many others do not do so and add to the inventory of failed strategies. One of the significant developments of recent origin is the External Quality Assurance and HEIs in India differ greatly in their response to this development. While the highly rated institutions have been successful in implementing EQA strategies, many others are still hesitant to volunteer for accreditation. While the general conditions governing all the institutions remain almost the same, why is one institution distinctly different from the others, in its success with EQA? This chapter analyses the aspects on which the highly rated institutions have been found to be different.

It is expected that most of the universities will undergo assessment by the end of 2002 and at least 25 per cent of the colleges by the end of 2003. This projection and expectation may present a rosy picture, but the current data is not all that good, at least in the case of colleges. The UGC circular indicating that a part of the development will be given only to accredited universities has pressurised the universities to volunteer quickly. The UGC circular also gives the deadline to get accreditation as December 2002 and consequently, as of October 2002, seventy universities out of around 160 liberal arts and science universities have been accredited. But in the case of colleges, out of nearly 12,600 colleges, only 226 — less than 2 per cent — have been accredited so far. Such a situation may tempt anyone to ask two questions:

(*a*) While the societal demands require EQA to be adopted by all the institutions of higher education, why is it that it has been accepted only by a few and not all?

(*b*) At the practical plane, only a few institutions are successful in implementing EQA strategies. While the general conditions governing all the institutions remain almost the same, why is one institution distinctly different from the others, in its success with EQA?

The Highly Rated Institutions (HRI)

The questions listed above have always been there from the very beginning. Initially NAAC thought, if the need for external quality assurance were made clear to the academia, the acceptability would improve. This assumption became true in the case of a group of institutions and the rest stated various hypothetical issues as defence mechanism. NAAC's practical experience proved that those who accepted NAAC did so not only because they were convinced and had faith in the process, but over and above that they were more organised and were confident of themselves to meet external scrutiny. Once that came to the forefront NAAC started looking for patterns that could be unique to these institutions.

students and parents for new programmes, many of the highly rated institutions, amidst all these debates, have introduced self-sustaining programmes, but with a difference. While those who can afford to meet the educational cost pay for it, the other deserving students, to the tune of 50 per cent of those admitted into such courses, are supported through various freeships and concessions. In Tamil Nadu, the State Government has fixed the fee structure for self-financing courses. But some of the highly rated institutions charge much less than the government fixed tuition fee and they do not turn down deserving students for want of money. If deserving, the students are accommodated under the scholarship scheme and more such schemes are being initiated with the support of new Endowments, Parent-Teacher Association and Alumni contributions.

Some of them have even taken-up the exercise of holding consultations to review their objectives and evolve a plan of action document in an organised way, involving the external experts. St. Agnes College of Mangalore organised a series of workshops to reflect on its goals. Lady Doak College of Madurai organised a national level consultation. University of Roorkee has evolved its Vision-2020; Birla Institute of Technology and Science (BITS) of Pilani has its strategic planning and the All India Association of Christian Higher Education (AIACHE) had a three days workshop to evolve specific goals for its member institutions. Further, the efforts of the Principal and faculty members of these institutions striving hard with a determination to meet goals and objectives set for the institution are highly commendable and the programme offerings by these institutions truly reflect the institution's mission, goals and objectives.

These initiatives are in contrast to what could be observed in a few other institutions. While browsing through the prospectus of the university, which NAAC visited recently, the NAAC officer noticed that the institution had introduced three new programmes that year. The objectives of the university very clearly spell out its commitment to promote integrated courses in humanities and sciences but none of the newly started courses were of integrated nature. Assuming that the institution might have discussed the merits and demerits of the integrated programmes and then opted for the conventional ones, the NAAC staff enquired whether there was any discussion about the goals and objectives while planning the new but conventional courses. The members of the faculty gave a puzzled expression and later criticised that NAAC used jargons which were either impractical or trivial. That university has perceived the expectation that an institution should be aware of its goals and initiate action towards reaching it, as impractical.

2. *Going Beyond the Minimum*

Establishing some healthy practices beyond the framework prescribed by the University, overcoming the systemic constraints imposed by the affiliating structure, has been observed in the HRIs. While many institutions give a list of reasons to justify why they are not doing what they are expected to do, these highly rated institutions have invented mechanisms to go beyond the perceived constraints.

Many affiliated colleges get into the mode of blaming the parent university for all the ills in the quality of education they provide. *'While the curriculum is framed by the university and examination is conducted by the university, what freedom do the affiliated colleges have?'* is the question raised very often. On the other hand, the university may feel that it is the affiliated colleges that decide the curriculum through their representation in the Board of Studies and it is the affiliated colleges who help in the examination process through the services of their faculty as either question paper setters or examiners. Hence, the university has a genuine right to say that it is not fair to simply blame the university mechanism but the faculty who render their services should also take some amount of responsibility to set the mechanism right. However, leaving apart these contentious debates, the HRIs have turned the very 'affiliation structure' to their advantage.

They look at the affiliating function of the university as a facilitating mechanism by which the parent university shoulders the responsibility of curricular aspects including examination, enabling colleges to focus on 'curricular transaction'. While the minimal requirement and threshold levels are ensured by the regulatory mechanisms of the university, these institutions have made their 'curricular transaction' very effective by enriching the syllabus, taking the university syllabus as a minimum base. Some institutions offer additional courses to enrich the student experience and to challenge faculty and students to go beyond the syllabus. St. Xavier's College of Mumbai, an affiliate of Mumbai University offers various courses for its students in the afternoon after regular working hours, without cutting into the university programmes. On fulfilling the requirements of the course, apart from learning a skill or subject of their interest, the students get a certificate awarded by the college, which is valued high by the job market and hence gives a competitive edge to the students of this college.

Though not a requirement by the University, the faculty members have used innovative evaluation techniques such as seminars, quizzes, assignments, project works, *viva voce* tests etc. for continuous assessment of students. The performance in the tests is discussed with students and thus evaluation procedures are made clear. Whenever necessary the parents are informed of student's progress.

In the case of autonomous institutions, introduction of cafeteria model of Choice Based Credit System (CBCS), introduction of semester pattern with continuous internal assessment, reforms in the examination system, assessment based on group discussion, model interviews, and *viva voce* exams, double valuation system at UG level also, development of Question Bank in a scientific way, the computerization of the examination branch and the efficient processing of the results have been observed. Some of them have made a provision to supply photocopies of the answer papers on payment, on the basis of which the students decide the need for revaluation or recounting. The dynamism of the highly rated autonomous institutions in introducing new courses to make education relevant to the needs of the students and society has been found to be commendable. Initiation, review and redesign of programmes are found to be systematic. Feedback on programmes from students has been a regular feature. Interaction with academic peers and employers has played an important role in initiating, redesigning and review of programmes in the highly rated autonomous institutions.

3. Enriched Educational Experience

Most of these institutions provide all possible avenues for a rich student experience in the campus — rich in terms of ample opportunities towards more participative, active learning environment. Use of new technology in teaching through introduction of audio-visual aids, group discussions for communication skills and self-study techniques for better learning have been observed in these institutions. Internships, on-the-job experience, projects, student seminars, subject association activities, journal clubs, study circles, co-curricular activities and leadership training enrich the student experiences.

Some colleges have introduced a compulsory course on value education for all students irrespective of their faith, covering self-awareness, personality development, duties towards God, family, neighbour, self, country, society etc. This helps the students to develop their personalities as whole human beings with the spirit of dedication to duty and as free citizens. Participation in NSS or Physical Education is a compulsory course requirement in many of these institutions, which moulds the students into responsible citizens with the realisation of their social responsibility.

To meet the specific requirement of students preparing for the various competitive examinations the faculty not only enriches the syllabus to facilitate the preparation for the entrance examinations, but also organise study circles and discussion groups. The toppers in the various fields are brought in, to share their experience with the students. These initiatives enable the advanced learners to be more competent to face the challenges of their career option.

Establishing national and international linkage through Memorandum of Understanding (MoU) with institutions of importance for faculty and student exchange and sharing of advanced facilities, inviting scholars/research scientists/experts from other institutions to deliver lectures on occasions to keep up academic interest among the students and teachers have been noticed in top institutions.

4. *Student at the Centre*

These institutions take care of the overall development of every individual and pay personal attention to students. Effective tutor-ward system, personal and academic counselling, placement cell, good hostels, and physical facilities for student activities are a few to name. The tutor-ward system that is followed in some of the HRIs needs a special mention wherein every teacher is allotted a small group of students. In the beginning of the academic year every tutor meets the wards regularly, say once a week, during specified periods allotted in the timetable. The meetings may become more or less frequent, depending on the needs of the students. The tutors pay personal attention to the academic and personal guidance needs of their wards.

Adequate financial assistance to the needy students with appropriate checks is found in these institutions. For example all the management scholarship holders in a particular institution should satisfy the condition of 75 per cent attendance and 'not having arrears' in every semester lest they forfeit their right for scholarship. The financial assistance is also given in the form of loan scholarships to enable economically backward students to pursue education.

These institutions have been able to inculcate a sense of discipline among the students. Instances of student unrest are rare, perhaps due to the variety of activities that help students spend their leisure time in a constructive way. Activities are planned to cater to the needs of individual learners. While the campus life is enriched with value added components for the advanced learners, the educationally disadvantaged are helped through bridge/remedial courses. Activities are not only planned to suit the learners, but also redesigned. Many of these institutions collect feedback from students, mostly formally and at an institutional level, on students' educational experience. It covers aspects like the curriculum, teacher preparedness, learning support, improvements that may be implemented in the teaching-learning process and campus facilities. The feedback collected from students is analysed and used to initiate strategies to improve the educational experience of the students.

Using student feedback has always been a bone of contention. NAAC has come across many faculty members who are sceptical about collecting feedback from students. The major objections are on the following lines:

(*a*) Do students have the ability to judge their teachers?
(*b*) If the students do not have a liking for a particular subject, perhaps due to its high difficulty level, will it not be reflected in their feedback on the teacher who handles that subject?
(*c*) As practitioners in this field, we know what is good for our students. How can we take the inexperienced students' feedback seriously to redesign their educational experiences?

The abovementioned questions are based on the wrong assumption that students are going to evaluate the teachers. It is true that the students may not be the right judges to assess their teachers. But they are the most appropriate persons to voice out "their educational experience". As a part of their experience, it is but natural that they may record about the teachers also. But the focus is not the teacher but the 'self' and the students have every right to express it. While the non-performers are caught in this mess of suspicion, the HRIs have been silently using this as an effective tool for self-improvement. Their experiences indicate that students have been genuine in their evaluation on the soundness of the curriculum, appropriateness of learning experiences, expectations towards campus life facilities, preparedness of the teachers etc. There may be one or two deviations but they are minimal.

In fact, some of these institutions have a high estimation of the potential of their students and think that the student feedback keeps them in touch with the fast changing present and be prepared for a more dynamic future. In their opinion, an institution that fails to respect the genuine expectations of the students will continue to have its foundation on theories of the past and will soon become obsolete. If an institution thinks that its students are not competent enough to evaluate their own educational experience, it is time that such institutions start preparing their students to be more responsible lest the institutions would be failing in their duty to mould responsible citizens.

Another important feature of the HRIs is the effective and functional grievance redressal and welfare schemes — both formal and informal. The operational mechanism of the institution is geared to facilitate student welfare and for solving the student grievance with minimal procedural bottlenecks. It does not mean that there are no grievances. But the grievances are sorted out without too much of hardship and delay and the student welfare is always at the centre.

5. High Faculty Profile

Normally institutions complain about two things — lack of adequate number of teachers and lack of qualified teachers who can handle the programme offerings. The government is blamed for not filling up the vacancies and also for not sanctioning additional teaching positions for new programme offerings. The locational disadvantage and relatively low salary compared to a few other avenues of a particular subject are mentioned as reasons for lack of 'adequately qualified teachers'. But with similar contextual conditions and systemic constraints, the HRIs have taken care to bring in well trained, qualified and adequate faculty members. They do not compromise on anything that may affect the quality of the institution. Though the number of teachers in a few of those institutions needs to be strengthened, apart from the optimal sharing of workload, care has been taken to rope in the support of the Alumni, Parents and Guest Lecturers. There is an overall co-ordination towards the common agenda of not letting the students to suffer at any cost. Faculty members, whether regular or guest faculty, whether they get a full pay or on hourly basis, have a sense of learning, growing, developing and also in contributing to the institution. The faculty members wish to stay with the institution, want to be influenced by it and have influence on it. The identification with the institution is visible.

The members have the feeling of well-being or satisfaction. Those who work well feel that they are happy and safe in the institution and there is mutual trust and freedom. This is mainly because of the distortion free open channels of communication among the faculty and management, which promotes team spirit and innovations. The faculty can influence upwards and can see that their Heads do the same with their superiors. The faculty members of the institution stand united and the 'small differences' are forgotten when they work with inter-dependent relationship to one another. They work as a team with less emphasis upon the ability of one person to control the entire operation in a nutshell. The faculty profile can be defined as individually competent and collectively productive and cohesive, bound by team spirit and institutional affinity.

6. Close to Community

These institutions have a strong sense of commitment to social cause. As a result, teaching, research and consultancy have a bearing on their applicability to the society. In fact many good research and consultancy initiatives have come out of their concern for the immediate neighbourhood. Offering guidance and counselling services, soil testing, ground water resource management, better ways of marketing, solving the technical problems of small scale industries, helping the neighbourhood industries in recruiting personnel, organising skill oriented and professional courses are a few to name.

The extension activities are found to be fully geared towards the upliftment of the community. In many institutions, putting in a particular number of hours of extension work becomes a course requirement. For example, the Science and Humanities for People's Development Programme of St. Joseph's College, Trichy is an inter-disciplinary academic requirement for all the students of the college. The objective is to expose all the students along with the faculty to understand the varied problems of the self-transformation of the rural people by taking up social, educational, developmental projects that would enable rural masses to become self-reliant.

More or less similar programmes and objectives may be found in many other institutions. But the meticulous way in which it is implemented in the highly rated institutions is noteworthy. Again to cite St. Joseph's College of Trichy as the example, to realise the objective of rural upliftment through 'academic requirement', the students are clubbed into 64 sections and each section has adopted a nearby village chosen on the basis of economical, educational and environmental backwardness. Each undergraduate and post-graduate student is expected to spend 100 and 80 hours respectively for this programme. 30 hours for undergraduates and 20 hours for post-graduates form the theoretical inputs and the remaining 70 hours for undergraduates and 50 hours for post-graduates will be in the form of various activities undertaken by students in the assigned villages. Students interest, knowledge and understanding, involvement and target achievement, team spirit, ability to communicate, initiative, creative ability etc. are constantly monitored and evaluated. The students of a particular section always stick to the assigned village till the completion of the programme. Similar noteworthy efforts have been observed in Ramnarain Ruia College of Mumbai.

While the institutions fulfil their social responsibilities, the society also supports the performing institutions appropriately. It is a two-way relationship beneficial to both ends. One could find a close link between the HRIs and the Alumni and Parent–Teacher Associations. Continuous parent-teacher interaction takes place to exchange views about the overall functioning of the institution. The Alumni Association is also actively involved in supporting the overall functioning of the institution. To some extent, this helps institutions to overcome the resource crunch. While they may not enjoy the luxury of surplus budget, at times of financial struggle the support of the society always comes to them handy, especially through Parent-Teacher Association and Alumni Association. Creation of a corpus fund with generous contribution from these associations for selected development activities with total judicious discrimination is also noted.

7. Quality Culture

Although quality assessment has been a world-wide phenomena from the past decade or so, even now questions are raised about the need for and relevance of NAAC. Ironically, most of these questioning institutions, do not even have an effective 'internal mechanism' to steer their self-improvement. In contrast, many of the HRIs have in-built checks and balances apart from the routine regulatory mechanisms to assess their functioning.

In institutions like St. John's Academy of Health Sciences, Bangalore and St. Xavier's of Mumbai NAAC found that inviting an external group once in 5 to 10 years to assess their functioning has been in practice since inception. In some institutions, analysing the performance by an internal committee has been a formal mechanism. In the other HRIs, the already existing informal mechanisms for quality enhancement facilitated the adoption of NAAC's suggestion to establish the Internal Quality Assurance Cell (IQAC) which is a formal mechanism. All these institutions had some element of 'Quality Culture' already existing and they found NAAC's methodology to be a more organised, systematic, external, objective and facilitating mechanism of national credibility. This enabled them to become 'national players' whereas the other institutions are not too sure about their own quality culture.

For example, when many institutions were questioning the advantages/benefits of undergoing Assessment and Accreditation, looking for extrinsic incentives like linkage with funding, deemed university status and fee structure, the HRIs accepted it for intrinsic values like self-analysis and self-improvement through peer review. In the decision-making, the administrative bodies provided active support rather than remaining neutral.

This quality culture has resulted in better ability to cope with change. The highly rated institutions are realistic and effective in their efforts to implement changes. It does not imply that they do not have problems in managing change but the manner in which they cope with changes is effective. Problems are solved with minimal energy, they stay solved and the problem-solving mechanisms are never weakened but maintained and strengthened. This is achieved mainly because they encourage a variety of contacts with outside sources and are willing to explore new ideas on their merit, regardless of the status of the immediate need and benefits. Higher financial support, high receptivity to current educational ideas, "open" climate, participation of students, faculty and staff in decision-making, excellent inter-personal relationships and good leadership have been nurtured over the years. In a nutshell, what NAAC propagates as critical elements that contribute to quality in education, have evolved over the years into a tradition in these institutions making them unique.

Getting 'social accreditation' by showing high student pass rate and student achievement in competitive examinations alone has been the driving force for many potential institutions for a long time. But, the changing context demands institutions of a new order — dynamic, vibrant, quality conscious institutions that can assure the quality of the output — students, in various dimensions of the job setting and social context. To relate themselves efficiently to this changing scenario it becomes imperative for the institutions of higher education to reflect on the seven aspects discussed above and see for themselves where they stand in comparison to the Highly Rated Institutions, which stand out on these aspects.

12 Towards Mutual Recognition

The International Agenda

In the context of globalisation of economies, technologies, communications and job market there is an increased mobility of knowledge seekers and educated workforce across the national boundaries. Quality assurance, accreditation and licensure are therefore of increasing importance to international efforts in standard setting and academic recognition. There have been several attempts in the past to evolve a suitable model for recognizing the qualifications awarded by an institution located in a particular country to facilitate the mobility of the students and workforce across the boundary. In this chapter, an attempt is made to trace the brief survey of the attempts made in this regard since the Second World War through successive institutional, national, regional, cross-regional and global systems of academic recognition which have ultimately culminated into greater reliance on the national external quality assurance agencies and their processes. In addition, a brief history of the emergence of transnational education and the related recognition systems are discussed. Finally, what the national EQA agencies and their international network can possibly contribute to this emerging need for mutual recognition across the national borders in the context of higher education becoming an international service is highlighted.

Early Attempts on Recognition

Traditionally, the academic recognition was given after establishing equivalence of the award gained by a student or a worker with similar programmes of the host country. Equivalence was established on the basis of the number of years of schooling (or the years spent at the tertiary institutions) and by assessing the extent of the similarity of the content of the courses studied with those of the domestic programmes. It was mostly done at the institutions on case-to-case basis. Most universities had established an academic recognition cell/ centre within their campus for this purpose. These centres were usually manned by senior academics from the foreign affairs office of the large universities who are knowledgeable about the course contents in the subject. Such methods were adequate when the number of inter-country migration was relatively small. When the demands for such recognition increased and when such demands came with a diverse background, there was a growing concern about the adequacy of the system of establishing equivalence based only on the number of years of study and the course contents. University based recognition centres within a country with conflicting yardsticks created more problems than solutions. Consequently national level single recognition mechanisms emerged virtually in all the countries of Europe in a variety of names and structures such as National Academic Recognition Centres, National Equivalence Information Centres, National Information Body, and Central Office for Foreign Education or World Education Services. They were functioning either at ministerial offices or at anyone of the large universities with a number of skilled staff who knew foreign languages well.

Very soon these national recognition centres felt the need for international co-operation among themselves. Bilateral agreements for such collaborations were signed between countries, like Austria, Germany, and Switzerland whose populations were bilingual. A little later, multinational co-operation became necessary. The European Network of

Information Centres on Recognition and Mobility (ENIC) is a typical multinational agency which served the member countries. Similarly, east European countries also established their network. After a while, the separate East and West European Recognition bodies were replaced by pan European centres. Network of National Academic Recognition Information Center (NARIC) established in 1984 by the European Community is a typical example of such pan European centres. Besides these developments many agencies such as European Credit Transfer System (ECTS) that provided academic and professional recognition within the European Union, were established to provide mutual recognition. In order to enable these systems in according the recognition, extensive databases were established throughout Europe. Trans Regional Academic Mobility and Credential Evaluation (TRACE) develped by NARIC is one of them. Later, higher education information system established in 1989 was co-ordinated by the International Association of Universities (IAU), an affiliate of UNESCO. European Association for International Education (EAIE) a non-governmental organization established in 1989 is an improved version of such multinational units for Academic Recognition. This was supported by the co-operation of the members of the National Association of Foreign Student Advisers (NAFSA). This continental — but multinational—outfit, became a trans-Atlantic recognition centre to serve the needs of European and American citizens with the help of the members of NAFSA drawn from both the continents. Trans European Exchange and Transfer Consortium (TEXT) is another non-governmental agency based at the University of Derby in UK. They have established an elaborate criteria and procedures in several stages of discussions in multinational conventions and working groups among inter-governmental organizations such as Council of Europe, UNESCO and European Communities/ Unions. The emergence of this inter-continental co-operation was an indication of the growing need for a truly international service for Academic Recognition.

American Experience

As in Europe, the United States of America had also to cope with growing demands for Academic Recognition. Their National Council for the Evaluation of Foreign Academic Credentials established in 1955 had produced placement recommendations for use by the American admission community through professional and centralised mechanism for establishing the equivalence. With the changes in the perception as to what should form the basis of according recognition along with the ever-increasing rush for getting certifications from an authentic agency, the attention of the council was focused on the quality and consistency of the credentials of the evaluation process. The methodology was modified and a set of benchmark for comparability between credentials of American awards and foreign qualifications were evolved through both national and multinational conventions. In addition, the American academia was in constant touch with the trends in Europe and elsewhere. This includes their active involvement with the continental efforts, like European Association for International Education (EAIE) and NAFSA. The challenges faced and solutions evolved by the Americans in this regard were not substantially different from those of the Europeans.

Indian Experience

India has the second largest network of higher education institutions catering to nearly seven million students with nearly 13,000 universities and colleges. A big country, bigger than the size of all the west and east European countries put together in area and much bigger in their population has about 30 States which support and regulate higher education in their respective States, independent of each other. Consequently, the awards and qualifications of the different State Universities and Colleges are quite variable in many ways. Inter-state migrations were limited because of these variations in the early decades of the post-Second World War era. Equivalence of the academic programmes was established, whenever such necessity arose and mostly in the professional area, at the institutional level through statutory committees. The use of such recognition is only for furthering their academic qualifications and not for the use of job market. After a while, the institutional arrangements were found inadequate and therefore, a centralised mechanism was evolved through an Equivalence Centre located at the Association of Indian Universities (AIU) office, New Delhi. It was manned by a few experts who, based on some database, would issue a certificate of equivalence. Since this centre was not adequate to serve the volume of demands that grew, after a decade or so, all the full member universities of AIU agreed formally to mutually recognise the awards of each other on a reciprocal basis. This agreement was based on the fact that AIU has stipulations and criteria for any university to become its full member, including a mandatory team visit to assess the institution for its eligibility. There was no special mechanism to screen the foreign awards except for the provision that some of the nearby countries like Sri Lanka, Nepal and Bhutan can become an associate member of AIU fulfilling their criteria and enjoy the automatic recognition of their awards.

Shift from National Recognition Centres to National Accreditation Systems

The developments in the area of Recognition in Europe, North America and elsewhere during the past 30-40 years, though predominantly concerned with the recognition of academic awards and qualifications, diversified into the area of professional and vocational studies as well. However, when the European academic recognition agencies had to extend their recognition to American awards, there were practical difficulties such as America's own system of quality assurance, *viz.* Accreditation. They had been practicing the system of Accreditation for ensuring the quality of education for almost a century. Their national and regional accrediting agencies accredited the institutions as a whole instead of awards and qualifications, except for the professional programmes that were evaluated along with the institutions with the help of one or more national or regional speciality councils.

With the massification of higher education in Europe and elsewhere and the consequent pressure on the recognition systems, they had to look for an alternative to the centralised recognition agencies. The American way of accrediting the educational institutions emerged as an obvious choice to ensure the quality of educational offerings. Subsequent developments in establishing National agencies for External Quality Assurance through assessment and accreditation all over the world including Europe, indicate how earlier practice of according recognition/mutual recognition had become outdated and even the signatories of the earlier conventions were unwilling to continue the practice. The factors that had contributed to this shift include the following:

(*i*) Emergence of the need for Recognition at pan European level.

(*ii*) Growth of a large number of non-governmental higher education institutions/universities everywhere.

(*iii*) Emergence of a large number of non-traditional programmes of study all over the world, particularly in US, Canada and UK.

(*iv*) Above all, the unprecedented growth of the overall size of the system of higher education as a whole.

Thus, based on the experiences of the past and the need to interactively recognize the awards of the North American continent on one hand and the east European and the rest of the world on the other, the world community had to shift its stand from heavy reliance on the centralised recognition systems and their variants. They have realised that the best way to source the requisite information for extending the recognition of the academic awards is to get it from the horses mouth, *viz.* from a quality assurance agency of the parent country from which the awards were given. However, it was also felt important to ensure that the agency has a clear and effective system for judging the quality of higher education in all institutions of its educational system. This perception had resulted in the greater reliance on national quality assurance agencies world over and the practice of using their accreditation as the basic criteria for the international recognition even though they may further be supplemented through appropriate speciality councils. After all, in any recognition of the awards and qualifications from an institution abroad, the question of quality is of paramount importance and these national agencies are best oriented to assure the same quality learning which cannot be described simply in terms of topics taught and examinations passed.

There were some reservations about relying completely on the recommendations of the national accrediting agencies and their instruments because these accrediting bodies were established in their respective countries with several objectives in mind. Many are designed to assess the institutional performance not only for the quality of educational offerings but also for their accountability to the stakeholders like the governments. Accountability concerns of the national accrediting agencies have very little to do with the international requirement of evidence for quality of educational awards. But this problem can be resolved if appropriate threshold indicators for quality are identified and used by the national EQA agencies in their instruments. There are quite a few models of threshold indicators available in literature. The major criteria in developing such indicators should mean that the institution/programme must include (1) clear and explicit aims and objectives, (2) human, financial and physical resources, (3) published curriculum in detail for the students to know what they are choosing, and (4) the institutional environment that is conducive for skill and competency development.

International/Transnational Education

Another recent phenomena is the emergence of transnational educational offerings by some national institutions for the benefit of the offshore students who seek quality education for moving into the international job market. Some of the international programmes offered by the developed countries to the developing countries tend to compromise on the quality and standards of their offerings and thereby attracting the criticism of not being fair either to their national standards or to the expectations of the receiving country. Therefore, quality assurance mechanisms for such transnational education become even more important. With the rapid growth over the last ten years of the number EQA agencies around the world, a new problem has emerged. If an institution in country A offers programmes in country B, should these programmes be subject to the external quality arrangement of country A or country B or both? The answer to this question is that if INQAAHE takes the initiative to facilitate the mutual recognition of the National Assessment and Accrediting agencies through some mechanism, the accreditation of the institution or the programme at the host country will be respected and there will be no need for the receiving country to repeat the process.

Possible Role of INQAAHE

A mutual recognition of the EQA agencies of a few contiguous countries or a region of the world or even the willing partners facilitated and ensured of their mechanisms by the INQAAHE will be one of the answers. The International Network of Quality Assurance Agencies in Higher Education should play a lead role in bringing an accord among the EQA agencies of the world through a set of initiatives including the accreditation of the accrediting agencies and encourage mutual recognition. This can be on the lines of Washington Accord by the Accreditation Board for Engineering and Technology (ABET) from US, the institutions of Engineering of Australia, the Canadian Council of Professional Engineers and a few more organizations from Ireland, United Kingdom, New Zealand, South Africa and Hong Kong. If the professional organizations could do it, INQAAHE can also take the initiative. After all the most important points on which the signatories are to agree for Washington Accord are nothing extraordinary or special. These are:

(*i*) The criteria, policies and procedures used by the signatories in accrediting institutions/programmes are comparable.

(*ii*) The accreditation decisions rendered by one signatory are acceptable to the other signatories and that those signatories will so indicate by publishing statements to that effect in an appropriate manner.

(*iii*) They should continue mutual monitoring and information exchange by whatever means are considered appropriate including:

   (*a*) Regular communication and sharing information on the criteria, systems, procedures, manuals and other publications and the list of accredited units,

   (*b*) Invite accord partners to observe accreditation visits, and

   (*c*) Invite accord partners to observe their board and other important meetings where decisions on the accreditation are taken.

These stipulations are reasonable and INQAAHE can also adopt and implement them without much difficulty. Presently, in the absence of such efforts among the network agencies, other international bodies like Global Alliance for Transnational Education (GATE) and International Institute for Quality (IIQ) are taking the initiative.

GATE and IIQ

GATE and IIQ are emerging as multinational external (external to countries A and B) agencies for the purpose of assuring the quality of education offered by any country through a certification process quite similar to those of the national EQA agencies, but with international standards. The GATE Certification Manual notes that, "GATE's primary purpose is to address the assurance and improvement of the quality of education that crosses national borders". (GATE, 1999) The International Institute for Quality (IIQ) is the initiative taken by two international academic bodies — Quality Assurance International and CINDA — which are, in turn, dedicated to quality related issues. The IIQ manual indicates that "The International Institute for Quality is devoted to the assurance and improvement of quality in higher education through reviewing and accrediting institutions in relation to widely accepted international standards. The core services offered by the organisation are commissioned consultancies and independent institutional reviews against specified international standards." In these procedures, there are some modifications both in the criteria used and in the composition of the peer team that visits the institution to validate the claims. But a cursory survey of their processes would indicate that there is not much difference between their evaluation process and those of other national EQA agencies. In fact when they undertake the certification process of an international education programme that are designed for overseas clients, they involve the members of the other national accrediting agencies or their expert nominees who have wide experience in the accreditation process. Now GATE has moved away from mainstream to assess only electronic learning. As of now IIQ's certification process seems to be the only external review mechanism available to evaluate the transnational education.

However, the contribution of the transnational education is a minor one in this context. The bulk of it is drawn from the formal national educational systems of the respective countries. Therefore, the quality assurance of the national stream of education, with or without the overtone of internationalisation will have to play an important role in serving the stakeholders across the national boundary as well.

ISO Standards

Another approach that is emerging is the application of the ISO family of standards to assess the quality of the international education. ISO 9000 is the generic term for the ISO family of standards and guidelines relating to the quality assurance of management systems. ISO 9002 addresses management processes of the industrial houses originally but now suitably adopted to review the educational system. An elaborate process for ISO 9002 implementation in a university environment has been evolved and the outcome is expected to assure certain level of quality. A few educational institutions in India have already got the ISO certification through the national bodies that have the ISO membership, with a hope that their education would have worldwide recognition. However, the ISO members, in a recent development and on the advise of ISO, would be assessing educational institutions only after they have been accredited by the national EQA agencies like NAAC.

EQA Agencies and Their Role in Mutual Recognition of the National Education

It is true that the formal higher educational institutions of any country though nationally based, are no longer considered to be nationally bound. However, the national systems for quality assurance which are nationally limited in breadth and reach will not be enough and satisfying to assure quality to the international expectations. Historically the domestic process for quality assurance was not intended to serve international purpose. But now they have to serve the international stakeholders. How to resolve this conflict of interest of the national quality assurance agencies is the main issue. The major questions related to this issue are: Should national quality assurance systems pay more attention to the demands of international stakeholders? Should the quality assurance systems themselves be internationalised or should they be replaced by completely different mechanisms? Who should take the initiative and to have the responsibility?

Similarities Between EQA and IQRP Mechanics

Most of the EQA agencies across the world, now numbering

about 100 use the same basic sequence of processes in reviewing an institution or a programme with minor modifications. They include, self-assessment, peer review and their report, again based on certain basic criteria that are universally applicable. The joint collaborative project, Internationalisation of Quality Review Project (IQRP) specially undertaken to address the issues of the quality assessment and assurance of the institutional, international dimensions, in addition to the use of EQA instruments, supplemented criteria specially meant to evaluate the quality of the international aspects. They include, the institutional goal and the integration of international dimensions into the primary functions and priorities of the institutions. IQRP also used the same protocol, *viz.*, Self-assessment based on self-study report, peer review and peer team report as followed by EQA agencies world over. Therefore, if the national EQA agencies could use the experiences of the IQRP and improve with certain modifications of their instruments, they can very well serve the international stakeholders as well.

Possible Conditions for Mutual Recognition of National Accrediting Agencies

Vroeijenstijn has outlined in his paper entitled "Towards a Quality Hallmark for Higher Education and Towards Mutual Recognition of Quality Assessment Agencies" the conditions for mutual recognition between the National Accrediting agencies. (Vroeijenstijn, 1999) Similar critical criteria have also been used in the IQRP model to some extent. They are:

(*i*) The assessment should be carried out by an intermediate body that is independent from both the government and the Higher Education Institutes.

(*ii*) The assessment should be open and transparent based on fixed and clear guidelines.

(*iii*) It should be based on self-assessment and assessment by external experts. If possible not only national experts should be invited but also the foreign experts.

(*iv*) There should be a public report in which certain topics will be treated and a judgment of the quality will be given in a two or multi-point scale.

By and large all the members of the INQAAHE network will fulfil these basic conditions. If improvements were needed they would only be marginal. Therefore, there is case for taking the initiative to formalize the mutual recognition process either by following the Washington accord model or by any other suitable modality. It is time to move.

From the survey of history of the development of the policies and practices of academic recognition of degrees and awards one can see how the interest gradually expanded to include the recognition of universities as institutions of higher learning, as both are closely related. Such academic recognition was also linked to the question of recognizing the private universities and other international education centres within a country. Thus the process of academic recognition that began at the awards and qualifications level gradually expanded to cover the institutions of higher learning as a whole, and gave way to the present day accreditation and quality assurance processes that is now universally adopted. The national agencies for quality assurance and accreditation are the key nodal points for any academic interaction internationally. INQAAHE can enhance their quality of function and status through constructive interactions, evolving accords and facilitating their role in mutual recognition of the institutions of higher learning throughout the world. The modalities can be worked out, if all agree on the principle of mutual recognition among national EQA agencies and the lead role INQAAHE should play.

Appendices

Appendix I: Criteria and Key Aspects

Criterion I: Curricular Aspects

- Compatibility of the programmes with goals and objectives
- Initiation, review and redesign of programmes
- Feedback on programmes and interaction with academic peers and employers
- Programme options

Criterion II: Teaching-Learning and Evaluation

- Judging students' knowledge and bridge/remedial courses
- Teaching-Learning process and use of new technology in teaching
- Co-curricular activities
- Examination process and innovative evaluation methods
- Recruitment of faculty and faculty development programmes
- Evaluation of teaching, research and work satisfaction of faculty and monitoring and rewarding successful teaching innovation
- Access to national and/or international linkages

Criterion III: Research, Consultancy and Extension

- Promotion and sustenance of research culture and research output
- Freedom to publish in academic forum and publication
- Benefits of consultancy to the institution and society
- Faculty participation in extension programmes and the

extension activities conducted so far
- Resources to conduct extension activities and service provided in the area of expertise

Criterion IV: Infrastructure and Learning Resources

- Physical facilities
- Maintenance
- Optimal use of infrastructure
- Library
- Computer facilities
- Laboratories
- Health services
- Sports and physical education
- Hostel, Canteen, Guest House
- Others

Criterion V: Student Support and Progression

- Progression to employment and further study
- Pass and dropout rate and student achievement
- Alumni association, its activities and alumni profile
- Financial aid to students
- Personnel and academic counselling
- Placement services

Criterion VI: Organisation and Management

- Organisation structure and functions and powers of functionaries
- Human power requirement and recruitment of staff
- Performance appraisal
- New technologies in communication
- Welfare schemes
- Grievance redressal mechanism
- Budgeting and auditing procedures
- Resource mobilisation and effective utilisation

Criterion VII: Healthy Practices

- Complementary System like self-financing courses, need-based courses
- National/International linkages for teaching and research
- Industry linkage
- Educational innovations such as credit system, examination reforms and modular curriculum
- Working with specific mission and goals
- Awards won by the faculty
- Others

Appendix II: Criterion Statements

Criterion I: Curricular Aspects

- The programmes of teaching and learning are consistent with the goals and objectives of the institution.
- Feedback from academic peers and employers is used in the initiation, review and redesign of programmes.

Criterion II: Teaching-Learning and Evaluation

- The programmes of teaching and learning cater to individual differences among learners and offers academic flexibility.
- The institution facilitates the effective running of the teaching-learning programmes.
- The evaluation procedures in the educational programmes are rigorous and fair.
- The regularity and the confidentiality of examinations are maintained.
- The institution has an efficient mechanism to recruit qualified and adequate faculty.
- The institution has an open and participative mechanism for evaluation of teaching, research and work satisfaction of the faculty.
- The faculties have opportunity for continued academic progress and professional advancement.
- The institution has a transparent admission process.

Criterion III: Research, Consultancy and Extension

- The institution promotes research culture among faculty and students.

- The institution has a vigorous and well scrutinised publication programmes and actively encourages faculty and students to publish in academic forum.
- The institution promotes faculty participation in consultancy work.
- The institution is responsive to community needs and conducts relevant extension and awareness programmes.

Criterion IV: Infrastructure and Learning Resources

- The institution has adequate library and computer facilities with easy access to all its constituencies.
- The institution has adequate physical facilities to run the educational programmes and administrative functions efficiently.
- The growth of the infrastructure keeps pace with the academic growth of the institution.
- The institution has effective mechanisms for maintenance and optimal use of infrastructure.

Criterion V: Student Support and Progression

- The institution has sufficient and well-run support services to ensure the physical and intellectual health of all its constituencies.
- The institution has an effective mechanism to use student feedback for the quality enhancement.
- The prospectus of the institution gives clear guidance to students about admission and completion requirements for all programmes, the fee-structure and refund policies, financial aid and student support services.
- Financial aid to students is fairly distributed.
- The institution offers competent academic counselling and placement services to its students.

Criterion VI: Organisation and Management

- The offices and departments of the institution are

governed on the principles of participation and transparency.

- Academic and administrative planning in the institution move hand in hand.
- Management techniques and technologies, to the extent possible, are used by the institution for efficient running of every administrative and academic decision-making.
- The institution practices relevant welfare schemes for all its constituencies.
- There are fair and expeditious grievance redressal mechanisms at all levels of the institution's functioning.
- The finances of the institution are judiciously allocated and effectively utilised to make its programmes and functioning cost-effective.
- The institution has imaginative and effective resource mobilisation and management strategies.
- Budgeting and auditing procedures are regular and standardised.

Criterion VII: Healthy Practices

- The goals and objectives of the institution are clearly stated, periodically reviewed, and communicated systematically to all its constituencies.

Appendix III: Pointers of Quality for Autonomous Colleges

I : Curricular Aspects	Credit points	
1. What is the range of programme options available to the students for awards such as degrees, certificates and diplomas?	For every 5 programme options	1 not exceeding 8 points
2. To what extent are the programme options career oriented?	>10% of the programmes	1
3. Are programmes flexible enough to offer students the following benefits?	Peer judgment, satisfactory for each aspect not exceeding 2 points	1
(a) Time frame matching student convenience and horizontal mobility		
(b) Elective options/Non-core options		
4. How often are the existing curricula for a subject reviewed and updated?	Peer judgment, satisfactory	1
5. What is the mechanism for formulating the curricular content of new programme?	Peer judgment, satisfactory	1
6. How long does it take to introduce a new programme of study after it is conceptualised?	Up to two years	1
7. What are the new programmes introduced by the institution during the last two years?	Peer judgment, satisfactory	1
8. What percentage of the members of the Boards of Studies, or such academic committees are external to the institution?	>20%	1

9.	Are there other strategies to review academic programmes besides the Academic Council ? If yes, how are such reviews made?	Peer judgment, satisfactory	1
10.	To what extent, laboratory work, fieldwork and projects are incorporated in each of the programmes of study?	Peer judgment, good Satisfactory	2 1
11.	How are the mission and goals of the institution, if any (other than the general transmission and generation of knowledge), reflected through the curricula?	Peer judgment, good Satisfactory	2 1
12.	Furnish details on the inter/multi-disciplinary approach of the curriculum design.	Peer judgment, satisfactory	1
13.	Does the institution offer any programme under the "self-financing" mode, recently encouraged?	Peer Judgment, satisfactory	1
14.	In what ways has autonomy facilitated the institution to achieve its objectives?	Peer Judgment, good Satisfactory	2 1

II : Teaching-Learning and Evaluation

1.	Furnish the following (a) working days of the institution, and (b) teaching days of the institution	 As per UGC norm As per UGC norm	 1 1
2.	What percentage of the total budget is allocated to the academic programmes? (other than salary component)	>3% 1% to 3%	2 1
3.	How are students selected for admission into various courses?	Peer judgment, satisfactory	1

No.	Question	Criterion	Score
4.	Apart from class room instruction, what are the other avenues of learning provided for the students? (projects, field training's, seminars, etc.)	Peer judgment, good	2
		Satisfactory	1
5.	Are there bridge/remedial courses offered for students?	Peer judgment, good	2
		Satisfactory	1
6.	Give the ratio of full-time teachers to part-time teachers (last two years).	>1	1
7.	What percentage of classes taught by full time faculty?	>50%	1
8.	What type of evaluation method is currently being followed and how long has it been in practice for?	Peer judgment, continuous and formative	1
		Revised within 5 years	1
9.	Are there guidelines for the selection of paper setters and examiners?	Peer judgment, established criteria exists	1
10.	What is the method of valuation followed?	Peer judgment, good	2
		Satisfactory	1
11.	What are the practices of the institution regarding the following? (a) double evaluation (b) moderation and adjustment of the pass/fail ratio (c) re-evaluation (d) re-totalling	Peer judgment, good	2
		Satisfactory	1

12. What is the time gap between the scheduled dates and actual dates in the conduct of examinations and announcing results?	Within 15 days from the schedule dates	1 for exams
	Within 15 days from the schedule dates	1 for results
13. How many of the academic faculty have at least a one-step higher qualification than the mandatory minimal level?	>50%	2
	25% to 50%	1
14. Give details about the number of teachers from the other institutions and from other states.	> 80% from other institutions	2
	50% to 80%	1
	>20% from other states	2
	10% to 20%	1
15. How do the faculty keep abreast with the recent developments in their subject area?	Peer judgment, good	2
	Satisfactory	1
16. Give the number of teachers who have attended seminars/ conferences/workshops as participants/resource persons in the last three years.	> 50% one activity during the last 3 years	2
	20% to 50%	1
17. How are the faculty inducted in the use of computer, information technology and such support services?	Peer judgment, satisfactory	1

18.	Does the institution follow self-appraisal method to evaluate teachers on teaching, research and work satisfaction? How the self-appraisal analysed and used?	Peer judgment, good	2 1
19.	Does the institution have a mechanism other than self-appraisal to evaluate teachers on teaching, research and work satisfaction? (peers, students, etc.)	Peer judgment, good Satisfactory	2 1
20.	Give details on a few faculty development programmes and the number of faculty who have benefited from it, during the last three years.	>10% 5% to 10%	2 1
21.	Indicate the number of faculty who have availed themselves of study leave and on duty leave for academic activities during the last three years.	Peer judgment, satisfactory	1
22.	In what ways has autonomy helped the institution in teaching-evaluation innovations?	Peer judgment, good Satisfactory	2 1

III : Research, Consultancy and Extension

1.	What percentage of the faculty are actively involved in research? (guiding research scholars, operating projects, publishing regularly etc.)	>30%	1
2.	Give details on the ongoing research projects.	>10% of the faculty	1
3.	Is there a separate research committee to facilitate and monitor research?	Peer judgment, satisfactory	1

4.	Furnish the following details : (a) research papers published at international and national levels (b) number of books published (c) number of Ph.D.s awarded during the last 5 years (d) number of research students currently registered for Ph.D. (full time and part time) (f) number of full time research scholars who have fellowships/scholarships (such as JRF/SRF, etc.) (g) awards/recognition for research work been given during the last 5 years	Peer judgment, satisfactory	1 for each aspect not exceeding 6 points
5.	Does the institution publicise the expertise available for consultancy services?	Peer judgment, satisfactory	1
6.	Give the broad areas of consultancy services provided by the institution during the last three years.	Peer judgment, satisfactory	1
7.	Give particulars of the finance generated through consultancy services by the faculty.	Peer judgment, satisfactory	1
8.	Does the institution have a designated person for extension activities?	Peer judgment, full time Part time	2 1
9.	What are the broad areas of extension activities?	Peer judgment, good Satisfactory	2 1
10.	Are there any outreach programmes carried out by the institution other than NSS and NCC, for example population education club, adult education, national literacy mission, or any other?	Peer judgment, satisfactory	1
11.	How are the students and teachers encouraged to participate in extension activities?	Peer judgment, good Satisfactory	2 1

12.	Does the institution work and plan the extension activities along with NGOs and GOs?	Peer judgment, satisfactory	1

IV: Infrastructure and Learning Resources

1.	Enclose the master plan of the campus indicating the existing buildings and the projected expansion in the future.	Peer judgment, good	1
2.	How does the institution plan to meet the need for augmenting the infrastructure to keep pace with academic growth?	Peer judgment, good	1
3.	How does the institution ensure maintain its infrastructure?	Peer judgment, good	1
4.	How does the institution ensure optimum use of its infrastructure facilities?	Peer judgment, good	1
5.	Give details on the following :		
	(a) number of working days of the library	>teaching days	1
	(b) working hours of the library	>teaching hours	1
	(c) advisory committee of the library		1
	(d) inter-library exchange	Committee exists	1
	(e) book bank facility	Peer judgment, satisfactory	1
	(f) computerisation of the library services	Peer judgment, satisfactory	1
	(g) ratio of library books to number of students enrolled	Peer judgment, satisfactory	2
		>40 vol./student	1
		20 to 40 vol./student	

No.	Question	Criterion	Points
6.	Give the cost of books/journals/periodicals that have been added to the central library in the last two years and their number.	> Rs. 5 lakh	2
		Rs. 1 lakh to Rs. 5 lakh	1
7.	Does the library provide the following facilities : (a) reprographic (b) computers (c) audio-video cassettes	Peer judgment, satisfactory for each facility not exceeding 3 points	1
8.	Give the following details about the central computer facility :		
	(a) configuration and other hardware and software	>20 terminals with updated software	1
	(b) working hours	7 to 10 hrs	1
	(c) output in developing computer aided learning packages	For every five CAL packages not exceeding 5 points	1
	(d) maintenance of computers		1
	(e) distribution of computer facility, number, use, software, etc.	Peer judgment, satisfactory	2
		Peer judgment, good	
9.	What are the physical and infrastructure facilities available in the sports and physical education centre?	As per UGC norm	1
10.	What are the physical and infrastructure facilities available in the workshop?	As per UGC norm	1
11.	What are the different welfare programmes of the institution?	Peer judgment, good	2
		Satisfactory	1
12.	Give details of the hostel facilities available in the campus.	>50% of the students	2
		10% to 50%	1

V : Student Support and Progression

No.	Question	Criterion	Score
1.	Furnish the following details :		
	(a) spread of students w.r.t. locale (same state, other state, NRI, overseas)	>10% from other states, NRI, overseas	1
	(b) pass % after the minimum period of study	>90%	1
	(c) dropout rate	<5% after 4 months	1
	(d) achievement of students in the competitive exams	>5% in national level	1
2.	Does the institution collect feedback from students regularly? How is the feedback obtained? How was it used last year?	Collected	1
		Analysed	1
		Used	1
3.	Are the contents of the prospectus updated annually?	Peer judgment, satisfactory	1
4.	How far the students get benefited from the academic and career counselling?	Peer judgment, good	2
		Satisfactory	1
5.	What kind of financial aids are available to students from central government, state government, the institution and others? and mention the number of students who have received for the last two years?	>10% students get financial aid of the unreserved category	2
		5% to 10%	1
6.	Does the institution have an employment cell and a placement officer who offers career-counselling to students?	Peer judgment, good	2
		Satisfactory	1
7.	To what extent do faculty participate in academic and personal counselling?	Peer judgment, satisfactory	1
8.	How many students were employed through placement services during the last year?	>5% of outgoing graduates	2
		2% to 5%	1

No.	Question	Criterion	Points
9.	Does the employment cell encourage the students to be self-employed? How many are self-employed?	>5%	2
		2% to 5%	1
10.	Does the institution have an alumni association? and what are the activities of the Alumni Association.	Peer judgment, good	2
		Satisfactory	1
11.	How are the prospective students informed clearly about the rules and regulations, facilities available, criteria for admission etc.?	Peer judgment, good	2
		Satisfactory	1
12.	Are the following support services given to overseas students : one window admission, special accommodation, induction courses, socio-cultural activities, welfare programme, etc.?	Peer judgment, good	2
		Satisfactory	1
13.	What are the recreational/leisure time facilities available to students in the campus?	Peer judgment, satisfactory	1
14.	Give details of the staff-structure, and facilities available in the health centre.	For health centre	1
		Permanent staff	1
		>10 beds with facilities	2
		5 to 10 beds	1
15.	Are the following health care facilities offered to students, faculty and staff? (a) Compulsory general medical check up (b) maintenance of health records (c) compulsory health insurance	For each aspect	1
16.	Are there quota in admission, and financial support given to students proficient in sports?	Peer judgment, good	2
		Satisfactory	1
17.	Give details of participation of students and the outcome, at the state, regional, national and international levels, during the last year.	For every participation at national/international not exceeding 5 points	1

VI : Criterion Organisation and Management

No.	Question	Criterion	Score
1.	Does the college have an efficient internal co-ordinating and monitoring mechanism?	If there is a mechanism	1
2.	Were any committees/external agencies appointed during the last three years to improve the organisation and management?	Peer Judgment, if yes	1
3.	Does the college have an in-built mechanism to check the work efficiency of the non-teaching staff?	If yes	1
4.	Is there a special committee for preparing the academic calendar?	If yes	1
5.	Does the college have a mechanism to monitor scheduled academic activities with rigour?	Peer judgment, If 80% activities adhered to schedule	1
6.	By and large have all the decisions of the selection committee/general body been approved?	Peer judgment, satisfactory	1
7.	Does the college conduct professional development programmes for non-teaching staff? Give details of the training programmes attended by the non-teaching staff	If yes	1
		Peer judgment, >50% benefited during last three years	2
		25% to 50%	1
8.	Has the college generated resources in the last year through the following sources : Donations, Fund raising drives, alumni association, self-financing courses	Peer judgment	
		>Rs. 1,00,000	2
		Rs. 25,000 to Rs. 1,00,000	1
9.	Furnish the amount spent under the various heads of expenditure last year.		
	(a) Percentage of expenditure on academic services	> 3%	1
	(b) Percentage of expenditure on administration and other common services	< 25%	1
	(c) Percentage of expenditure on student welfare services	>3 %	1

10.	Is there an internal audit mechanism?	If yes	1
11.	Tuition fee & changes in fee	For information	
12.	Is there a grievance redressal cell in the college? If yes, how does it deal with grievances of the employees and others?	Peer judgment, satisfactory	1
13.	Welfare schemes and loans.	Peer judgment, satisfactory	1

Glossary

12-b status: Recognition officially given by the UGC to an educational institution which makes it eligible for the grants of the commission.

2-f status: Recognition of an affiliated college accorded by the University Grants Commission.

Academic Audit: Official examination or review of academic performance.

Academic Bodies: Various statutory or other important bodies like Boards of Studies, Academic Planning Board, Academic Council, etc., which are responsible for academic decision-making.

Academic Calendar: The schedule of the institution for the academic year giving details of events and programmes like dates of reopening and closing, holidays, exams, results, convocation, etc.

Academic Growth: Enhancement of the teaching, learning, research and extension activities of the institution in quantity as well as quality.

Academic Unit: The academic department, or specifically defined subsection of a department with identified and defined responsibilities for curricular experiences. An academic unit generally has allocated faculty and physical facilities.

Accountability: Responsibility for satisfactory performance of one's duty.

Accreditation: The process of external quality review used in higher education to scrutinise institutions of higher education and their programmes for the quality of the educational provisions. Success results in an accredited institution and/or programmes. In the case of NAAC's accreditation, the period of validity is five years.

Affiliated College: A college that functions under the academic control of a university and the university legislates on courses of study and holds examinations centrally on common syllabi.

Assessment: A diagnostic form of quality review and evaluation of teaching, learning, and programmes based on a detailed examination of curricula, structure and effectiveness of the institution, its internal review, and quality control mechanisms.

Assessors: Trained specialists who are used to assess the unit of assessment.

Associate Member: An additional member of a body or team with limited rights.

Audit: A process of review of an institution or programme to determine if its curriculum, staff and infrastructure meet its stated aims and objectives. An audit focuses on accountability of institutions and programmes.

Autonomous Colleges: Colleges that have been conferred special status to design their curriculum and conduct examinations within the broad framework and the regulations of the parent university. However, the degree awarding power is vested with the university.

Beneficiaries: Those who stand to benefit from the outcome of an activity. For example, students, teachers, staff, employers, funding agencies, parents and society are stakeholders of accreditation.

Bridge Course: Courses designed for students who have general difficulties to cope with a curriculum owing to the sudden transition to a higher level of study. The bridge course is often of a short duration and it intends to bridge the gap between two levels of competence, one, present and the other, to be acquired.

Chairperson: An eminent educationist chosen to lead the Peer Team.

Choice Based Credit System (CBCS): A modular system whereby learners are often facilitated to make course choices and structure their programme of study. Performance is measured in terms of "Credit", *i.e.* "Credit hours" spent in learning a subject.

Co-curricular Activities: Activities which support the curriculum such as field trips, display of academic achievements (as in science exhibition) etc.

Community Orientation: Sensitisation of the activities of the institution towards the development of the immediate neighbourhood and the community at large.

Concurrent List: List of subjects dealt with by both the state and the central governments by constitutional provisions.

Education, for instance, is in the concurrent list of the Indian Government.

Conflict of Interest: The element of prejudice and personal bias, which may be in conflict with a free and uninhibited discharge of duty or function.

Constituent College: Colleges funded and managed directly by the parent university.

Consultancy: Activity with or without remuneration for which the expertise and the specific knowledge base of the faculty become the major input.

Counselling: Exhorting, assisting and guiding students individually or collectively for academic, career, personal and financial decision-making.

Course Completion Rate: Percentage of students in the total enrolment for the course who have satisfactorily completed all of the prescribed requirements of a given course.

Criteria: The set of predetermined well-defined basic features of functioning of an institution that forms the basis of evaluation and consequent decision making.

Curricular Aspects: Features of a curriculum – goal orientation, design, updating, relevance, practicability, flexibility etc. and the processes by which these are made possible.

Curricular Experiences: Planned, structured and formal teaching activities intended to enable students to learn and apply specific information, principles, values, and skills that are intended consequences of the formal education offered by an academic unit.

Deemed University: Deemed-to-be-universities are institutions that are conferred the status of a university by virtue of their tradition of teaching, or specialisation and excellence in a particular area of knowledge. The deemed university status is granted by the Department of Education, Ministry of Human Resource Development on the recommendation of the UGC.

Degree: An authorised recognition conferred by an approved educational institution acknowledging the satisfactory completion of a course of study or programme.

Departmental Accreditation: Evaluation of the functioning of the department of study taken as an independent entity with emphasis on subject *per se* in the backdrop of the institution as a whole.

Diploma: A document given by an educational institution

certifying the completion of a course of study.

Distance Education: Education process in which instruction occurs when the student and instructor are not located in the same place. Today Distance Education adds technology in many forms to the learning environment by a variety of means, such as web sites, e-mail, video conferencing and videotapes.

Documentary Evidence: Evidence adduced in the form of records.

Educational Objective: The statement of what a course or programme is expected to achieve.

Educational Records: Records and files maintained by an institution for each student's educational activity, which include the basic personal information about the student, date of enrolment, course combinations, grades, achievements, progress and other relevant information.

Elective Options: A choice available to the student to select from among a large number of courses of different orientation.

Enrichment Courses: Courses offered by the institution for student empowerment beyond the prescribed curricular contents. They often enrich the curriculum by amplifying supplementing and replacing such parts or features.

Entry-level: The preparation requirement considered necessary to enter a programme of study.

Evidence: Documentation that substantiates or verifies that the standard has been met.

Exit Meeting: The concluding session of the on-site visit in which the Chairperson of the Peer Team will share the highlights of the assessment, with the representatives of the institution.

Extension: The aspect of education that emphasises neighbourhood services. These may be either integrated with the curricula or be an extended opportunity to serve the community.

External Quality Assessment: Third party assessment made by the peers in the profession with pre-set criteria.

Faculty Development Programmes: Programmes meant for the updating of knowledge and pedagogical skills of the faculty.

Five-year Plan: Planned activities for the development of the nation designed by a Planning Commission. In the Indian context, the development plans are made for a period of every 5 years.

Format for Self-study: Structured pattern usually in the form of questionnaire evolved by NAAC to enable an institution to collect, compile and present data about the institution. This forms Part I of the Self-Study Report.

Globalisation: Expanded activities beyond the national limits.

Goal Focus: The helpful bias of an institution to achieve the set goals.

Grievance Redressal Cell: The body set-up for redressal of grievances of the constituents.

Gurukula System: Ancient system of education in India where masters and disciples spent an appointed period of time together. Learning was teacher-dependant but through creative interaction during the period of serving the teacher.

Handbook for Assessors: A manual of guidelines to Peers who undertake assessment.

Healthy Practices: Innovative practices of an institution that augment its academic quality.

Horizontal Mobility: The option for movement of student within and across disciplines.

Informal Mechanisms: Systems not codified or formally established which nevertheless achieve what formal systems do but with a greater degree of ad-hocism.

Infrastructure: Physical facilities like buildings, playfields, hostels etc. which help run an institutional programme.

In-house Analysis: A facilitating exercise made by the staff of NAAC to condense and highlight the various aspects of the self-study report and self-analysis meant for the use of the peer team during the assessment visit.

Input Indicators: Indicators concerned with the resources and factors employed in order to achieve the intended propose of the institution.

Institutional Accreditation: Evaluation of the functioning of an institution in its totality with its central governance structure and all its departments/centres.

Institutional Grade: Overall grade assigned to an institution for its total performance as a notional measure of accreditation.

Institution-industry Linkages: Formal agreement for the co-operation between an educational institution and industry/ industries generally, located in the neighbourhood. They are meant for mutual benefits such as consultancy, and vocational training, besides other.

Integrated Courses: Integrating two or more vertically

separated qualifications through appropriate redesigning of the curricula, to provide professional quality and competence in the related discipline.

Inter-team Variance: Difference in perceptions of quality between Peer Teams.

Internships: Students serving as trainees in professional houses such as banks, hospitals and companies as a partial fulfilment of the award requirements.

Key Aspects: Focal features substantially central to a given standard of assessment.

Learning Resources: Those that help learning – material resources include infrastructure and human resources include mentor counsel and guidance.

Licensure: Certification given by a professional body to a qualified individual to practice his profession.

Linkage: A formal agreement/understanding between any two or more institutions for training/student exchange/faculty exchange or research through a memorandum of understanding or such procedures.

Manual for Self-Study: Document that details the process of preparing the Self-Study Report.

Massification: Quantitative expansion to provide access to a large body of beneficiaries.

Master Plan: Long-term planned projection of the institution's path of growth.

Meta Evaluation: Evaluation of evaluation systems and processes.

Mid-term Review: Review of performance mid-way during a programme or an academic calendar.

Modular Curricula: Courses offered in smaller units covering one or more related concept that are complete in themselves.

Multi-faculty University: A university with more than one faculty of study.

Multinational Conventions: Conference or a meet meant for or organised by several nations.

Mutual Recognition: Agreement between any two institutions to recognise their processes, products and programmes as mutually valid.

National Panel of Assessors: Panel of assessors generated by NAAC through formal training.

Ninth Plan Document: Document outlining the ninth five-year plan.

Non-merit Item: An economic jargon indicating the inputs that do not bring economic returns.

On-site Visit: Actual visit to an institution by the Peer Team.

Open Climate: Free atmosphere conducive to pursuits without inhibition.

Organisation and Management: Systematic governance and administration of the institution.

Outcomes: The results of instruction such as employment, measurable gains in competency, increased knowledge, skill and attitude.

Output Indicators: Signals that reveal the impact of performance (the number of students of an institution who successfully clear competitive exams, for instance).

Outstanding Issues: Concerns identified by the review team that will be shared with the Head of the institution for clarification before the finalisation of the assessment report.

Overall Grade: Though peer assessment is at the criterion-level, the final out come is in terms of a single grade for the whole unit of assessment known as the overall grade which may include factors not fully covered by the analyses based on criteria alone.

Panel of Peers: The panel of experts from which a smaller number of experts will be chosen to constitute the Peer Team. This list will normally be sent to the Head of the institution to know whether the institution has any reservation against any of the members.

Peers: Experts in various fields of higher education who would assist NAAC in assessment of institutions. They are 'peers', being colleagues in the teaching profession.

Performance Indicators: Measurement for assessing the quantitative performance of the system.

Perspective Plans: Plans with future-focus.

Placement Cell: A unit of an educational institution that offers vocational counselling and organises facilities for employment to its graduates (campus interviews, for instance).

Process Indicators: Indicators related to the way in which resources and factors are combined and used in order to produce the institution's output.

Professional Bodies: Speciality councils and professional bodies that oversee quality of education and training in their respective areas of study. Medical Council of India is one such body competent to oversee medical education.

Programme Accreditation: Accreditation of any programme of study for a specific qualification, *e.g.* M.Sc., M.Tech., B.A. etc.

Programme Options: A range of courses offered at various levels leading to degrees/diplomas/certificates for students to choose from.

Progression: Vertical movement of student from one level of education to the next higher level successfully or towards gainful employment.

Quality Assessment: A diagnostic review and evaluation of teaching, learning, and outcomes based on a detailed examination of curricula, structure and effectiveness of the institution or programme. Designed to determine if the institution or programme meets generally accepted standards of excellence.

Quality Assurance: Planned and systematic review process of an institution or programme to determine that acceptable standards of education, scholarship, and infrastructure are being maintained and enhanced. Usually includes expectations that mechanisms of quality control are in place and effective. Also, the means through which an institution confirms that the conditions are in place for students to achieve the standards set by the institution or other awarding body.

Quality Audit: A test of an institution's quality assurance and control system through a self-evaluation and external review of its programmes, staff, and infrastructure. Designed to provide an assessment of an institution's system of accountability, internal review mechanisms, and effectiveness with an external body confirming that the institution's quality assurance process complies with accepted standards.

Quality Controls: Mechanisms, processes, techniques and activities necessary to ascertain whether a specified standard is being achieved.

Quality Improvement: The expectation that an institution will have in place a plan to monitor and improve the quality of its programmes. In most cases, quality assurance and accrediting agencies require that established procedures ensure that this is an ongoing process.

Quality: Refers to "fitness for purpose" — meeting o

conforming to generally accepted standards as defined by an accrediting or quality assurance body.

Question Bank: Collection of questions professionally framed by competent teachers that is updated and replenished periodically, for examining the student achievements. Often a question bank ceases to be one if the questions deposited do not mark a large number. The question paper setter is free to choose any form the collection

Remedial Instruction: Special instruction designed and delivered to alleviate deficiencies in basic skills needed to complete a course or programme.

Research: Probes into what is known to reach the unknown; it is often the rigour of inquiry which is accomplished by objective pursuit of knowledge.

Self-analysis: This is Part II of the self-study report that highlights the self-analysis in terms of strengths and weaknesses of the institution under the seven criteria. Part –I of the SSR forms the basis for this.

Self-appraisal: Individual's (or institution's) own evaluation of his/her (or its) performance.

Self-study Report: A report prepared by an institution after a careful study of its operations with reference to how it meets the standards of the accreditation agency. This is a pre-requisite for assessment and accreditation by NAAC.

Self-study: The review and evaluation of the quality and effectiveness of an institution's own academic programmes, staffing, and structure, based on standards set by an outside quality assurance body, carried out by the institution itself. Self-studies usually are undertaken in preparation for a quality assurance site visit by an outside team of specialists. Results in a self-study report.

Site Visit: Evaluation by a team of peer reviewers who examine the institution's self-study; interview faculty, students, and staff; and examine the structure and effectiveness of the institution and its academic programmes. Usually results in an evaluation. Normally part of the accreditation process, but may be initiated by the institution itself.

Standards: The level of requirements and conditions that must be met by institutions or programmes to be accredited or certified by a quality assurance or accrediting agency. These conditions involve expectations about quality, attainment, effectiveness, financial viability, outcomes, and sustainability.

Student Services: Supplemental activities and resources provided for students to assist them perform to their potential, motivate them and to respond to their needs — academic and non-academic nature.

Student Support: Facilitating mechanisms like guidance cell, placement cell and the financial aid given to students.

Subject Expert: A specialist in a particular field of knowledge.

Teaching–learning: The hyphen indicates that the two cannot be isolated. Learner centred pedagogy makes teaching subordinate to learning.

Team Report: The report of the evaluation resulting from a site-visit by reviewers of a particular institution or programme. Results in an accreditation or quality assurance recommendation or denial (an adverse action).

Tentative Evaluation: The evaluation made by the peers based on the Self-Study Report alone, before the on-site visit.

Unit of Accreditation: A college or a department or a university constitutes the 'unit' of assessment. The holistic observation, assessment and judgment underlies the meaning of the term.

University Level Institutions: Any institution that is empowered to legally confer degrees, but not designated as university.

Vertical Mobility: Moving up the academic or social ladder to perform higher tasks in the academic or social system.

Weightages: Taking cognizance of the different types of relationship between the colleges and universities, each of the seven criteria has been given a differential weightage in order to fairly distribute scores without any handicap, incidental to a particular type of affiliation, affecting fair judgment.

Bibliography

Advanced Education and Career Development (AECD) (1995), *A Proposal for Performance-based Funding*, AECD, Alberta Learning, Canada.

Advanced Education and Career Development (AECD) (1999a), *Key Performance Indicators Reporting Manual*, AECD, Alberta Learning, Canada.

Advanced Education and Career Development (AECD) (1999b), *System-wide Information Reporting*, AECD, Alberta Learning, Canada.

Advanced Education and Career Development (AECD) (1999c), *Revised Performance Envelope Model: A Discussion Paper Prepared for Consultation*, AECD, Alberta Learning, Canada.

Allsop P. *et al.* (1990), *Performance Indicators: The Development of Common Performance Indicators, Their Implementation and Critical Evaluation* (Final Report of a CNAA Development Fund Project), Portsmouth Polytechnic, UK.

Association of Indian Universities (AIU) (1995), *Policies of Higher Education*, AIU, New Delhi.

Association of Indian Universities (AIU) (2000), *Universities Handbook* - 28th edition, AIU, New Delhi.

Association of Universities and Colleges of Canada (AUCC) (1994), *Measuring up: Using Indicators to Manage Change*, Proceedings of 1993 AUCC Symposium, Ottawa.

Association of Universities and Colleges of Canada (AUCC) (2000), *Reach Higher: Choose a Canadian University*, AUCC, Ottawa.

Bloom, D. E. and Rosovsky, H. (2001), Higher Education and International Development, *Current Science*, 81(3), 252-256.

Bottrill, K. and Borden, V. (1994), Performance Indicators: History, Definitions and Methods, In Borden and Banta (Eds.) *Using Performance Indicators to Guide Strategic Decision-Making*, Jossey-

Bass, San Francisco.

Burge, S. E. and Tannock, J D. T. (1992), A New Approach to Assurance for Higher Education, *Higher Education Quarterly,* 46(1), 108-23.

Campbell, C. and Van der Wende, M. (2000), *International Initiatives and Trends in Quality Assurance for European Higher Education,* European Network for Quality Assurance, Helsinki.

Cave, M. *et al.* (1998), *The Use of Performance Indicators in Higher Education: A Critical Analysis of Developing Practice,* Jessica Kingsley, London.

Centro Interuniversitario De Desarrollo (CINDA) and Quality Assurance International (QAI) (2002), *Standards and Procedures Manual,* International Institute for Quality (IIQ), Washington DC.

Colleen, Liston (1999), *Managing Quality and Standards,* Oxford University Press.

Commission on Evaluation of Colleges (CEEC) (1994a), *Evaluating Institutional Policies on Programme Evaluation, Commission d'evaluation de l'enseignement collegial,* CEEC, Quebec.

Commission on Evaluation of Colleges (CEEC) (1994b), *Evaluating Institutional Policies on the Evaluation of Student Achievement, Commission d'evaluation de l'enseignement collegial,* CEEC, Quebec.

Commission on Evaluation of Colleges (CEEC) (1994c), *The Commission d'evaluation de l'enseignement collegial: Its Mission and Orientations,* CEEC, Quebec.

Commission on Evaluation of Colleges (CEEC) (1997), *Specific Guide to the Evaluation of Programme of Studies leading to a Diploma of College Studies in the Business Administration Technology and Cooperation Sectors,* CEEC, Quebec.

Committee of Vice-Chancellors and Principals (CVCP) (1985), *Report of the Steering Committee for Efficiency Studies in Universities* ('The Jarratt Report'), CVCP, UK.

Craft, A. (1992), *Quality Assurance in Higher Education,* Proceedings of the International Conference held at Hong Kong in 1991, The Falmer Press, Bristol.

Craft, A. (1994), *International Developments in Assuring Quality in Higher Education,* Proceedings of the International Conference held at Montreal in 1993, The Falmer Press, Bristol.

Cuenin, S. (1987), The Use of Performance Indicators: An International Survey, *International Journal of Institutional*

Management in Higher Education, 11(2).

Davis, D. (1996), *The Real World of Performance Indicators*, Commonwealth Higher Education Management Service, London.

Department of Education, Training and Youth Affairs (DETYA), (2000), *The Australian Higher Education Quality Assurance Framework*, DETYA, Canberra.

Desai, A. S. (1999), *Community Colleges*, Inaugural Address at the Seminar on Community Colleges, AIHSHEW, Coimbatore.

Doherty, G. D. (Ed.) (1994), *Developing Quality Systems in Education*, Routledge Publication, United Kingdom.

Frazer, M. (1996), Recognition: The Role of Quality Assessment Agencies, *Higher Education in Europe*, 30(4).

Gaither, G. H. (1996), The Assessment Mania and Planning, *Planning for Higher Education*, 24 (Spring), 7-12.

Gaither, G. H. (1997), Performance Indicator Systems as Instruments for Accountability and Assessment, *Assessment Update*, 9(1).

Global Alliance for Transnational Education (GATE) (1999), *Certification Manual: Assuring the Quality of Education and Training which Cross National Borders*, GATE, Washington DC.

Gnanam, A. (1999), *Quality Assurance*, Discussion Paper, South Zone Vice-Chancellors Meet, Pondicherry.

Gnanam, A. and Stella, A. (1998), Relevance of National Assessment and Accreditation Council in the Indian Context, *University News*, Association of Indian Universities, New Delhi, 36(51), 1-10.

Gnanam, A. and Stella, A. (1999a), Performance Appraisal as a Strategy for Professional Development, *Journal of Higher Education*, University Grants Commission, New Delhi, 22(1),133-141.

Gnanam, A. and Stella, A. (1999b), Emerging Trends in Higher Education and Their Implications for Future, *Journal of Educational Planning and Administration*, National Institute for Educational Planning and Administration, New Delhi, 13(2), 187-197.

Gnanam, A. and Stella, A. (Eds) (2002), *Quality Assurance in Higher Education: Quality, Standards and Recognition*, Proceedings of the INQQAHE-2001 conference, Allied Publishers, India.

Gordon, G. (1999), Creating Effective Internal Processes for Quality Assessment, Management and Development, *Assessment Update*, 11(6).

Government of India (GoI) (1986), *National Policy on Education - 1986*, New Delhi.

Government of India (GoI) (1992a), *National Policy on Education* (with modifications undertaken in 1992), Department of Education, Ministry of Human Resource Development, New Delhi.

Government of India (GoI) (1992b), *Programme of Action - 1986*, New Delhi.

Government of India (GoI) (1995), *Budgetary Resources for Education (1951-52 - 1993-94)*, MHRD, New Delhi.

Higher Education Funding Council of England (HEFCE) (1998), *About the HEFCE: An Introduction to the Work of the Higher Education Funding Council for England*, HEFCE, UK.

Holloway, J. *et al.* (Eds.) (1995), *Performance Measurement and Evaluation*, Sage Publications.

Imrie, B. (1998), Professional Development is Quality Assurance: Now and Zen, *Quality in Higher Education*, 4(3).

James, T. Rogers (1997), Assessment in Accreditation: Has It Made a Difference? *Assessment Update*, 9(9).

John, R.N. Bullivant (Ed.) (1994), *Benchmarking for Continuous Improvement in the Public Sector*, Longman Publications, London.

Johnes, J. and Taylor, J. (1990), *Performance Indicators in Higher Education*, The Society for Research into Higher Education and Open University Press, UK.

Joshi, M.M. (1998), *Higher Education in India: Vision and Action*, UNESCO World Conference on Higher Education in the 21st Century, 5-9 October 1998, Paris, www.education.nic.in/htmlweb/unhighedu.htm

Khan, A. W. (1999), Quality Assurance in Distance Education, In *Quality Assurance in Distance Education*, Powar, K. B. and Bhalla, V. (Eds.) (1999), Association of Indian Universities, New Delhi.

Knight, J. and Hans, de Wit (1999), An Introduction to the IQRP Project and Process, In *Quality and Internationalization in Higher Education*, Imhe Publication.

Lenn, M. P. (1996), The Globalisation of the Professions and Higher Education: Trade Agreements, New Technologies and the Quality Imperative, *Higher Education in Europe*, 21 (4), 89-96.

Massaro, V. (1996), Institutional Responses to Quality Assessment: Developing Diversity, *Journal of Higher Education Policy & Management*, 18(1).

Mathur, S. P. (1999), Designing of Performance Indicators for Universities: A Systems Approach, *University News*, Association of Indian Universities, New Delhi, 37(17).

McVicar, M. (ed.) (1989), *Performance Indicators and Quality Control in Higher Education*, Portsmouth Polytechnic, UK.

Meade, P. and Woodhouse, D. (2000), Evaluating the Effectiveness of the New Zealand Academic Audit Unit: Review & Outcomes, *Quality in Higher Education*, 6(1).

Morrison, H. G. *et al.* (1995), Performance Indicators and League Tables: A Call for Standards, *Higher Education Quarterly*, 49(2).

Nair, S. (1990), *Action Plan-cum-Project Report for Setting up the National Accreditation Board for Higher Education (NABHE)*, Project document submitted to University Grants Commission, New Delhi.

National Assessment and Accreditation Council (2000), *Memorandum of Association and Rules of NAAC*, NAAC, Bangalore.

National Assessment and Accreditation Council (2002), *A Profile*, NAAC, Bangalore.

National Assessment and Accreditation Council (2002), *Frequently Asked Questions and Answers on Assessment and Accreditation*, NAAC, Bangalore.

National Assessment and Accreditation Council (2002), *Institutional Accreditation: Manual for Self Study for Affiliated/ Constituent Colleges*, NAAC, Bangalore.

National Assessment and Accreditation Council (2002), *Institutional Accreditation: Manual for Self Study for Autonomous Colleges*, NAAC, Bangalore.

National Assessment and Accreditation Council (2002), *Institutional Accreditation: Manual for Self Study for Universities*, NAAC, Bangalore.

National Assessment and Accreditation Council (2002), *NAAC's Process of Assessment and Accreditation: How to go about*, NAAC, Bangalore.

National Informatics Centre (2002), *Educational Statistics*, online www.education.nic.in

Nigavekar, A. S. (1996), *Quest for Quality*, National Assessment and Accreditation Council, Bangalore.

Nilsson, K. A. and Wahlen, S. (2000), Institutional Response to the Swedish Model of Quality Assurance, *Quality in Higher Education*, 6(1).

Ontario Council on Graduate Studies (1996), *The Appraisals Process in Ontario*, OCGS, Toronto.

Panchamukhi (1999), *Indicators of Institutional Assessment in Higher Education: Some Conceptual Considerations*, Proceedings of the Bi-national Conference on *Quality Assurance in Higher Education: Criteria, Benchmarks and Indicators*, NAAC, Bangalore.

Powar, K. B. (1996), *Accreditation in Higher Education: An Indian Perspective,* Viva Books Private Limited, New Delhi.

Powar, K. B. (2000), *Reforms and Innovations in India: The Relevance and Role of Research*, AIU Occasional Paper 2000/1, Association of Indian Universities, New Delhi.

Powar, K. B. (2001), *Higher Education for Human Development in the 21st Century,* Association of Indian Universities, New Delhi.

Powar, K. B. (2002), *WTO, GATS and Higher Education: An Indian Perspective,* Association of Indian Universities, Occasional Paper 2002/1, Association of Indian Universities, New Delhi.

Powar, K. B. *et al.* (Eds.) (2000), *Performance Indicators in Distance Higher Education,* Aravali Books International Private Ltd., New Delhi.

Prakash, S. (1996), *Cost of Education: Theoretical Explorations and Empirical Prognostication,* Anamika Publishers and Distributors, New Delhi.

Quality Assurance Agency for Higher Education (1998), *Quality Audit Reports,* Quality Assurance Agency for Higher Education, UK.

Report of the CABE Committee on Policy (1992), Ministry of Human Resource Development, Government of India, New Delhi.

Report of the Committee on Review of National Policy on Education 1986 (1990), Department of Education, Ministry of Human Resource Development, Government of India, New Delhi.

Salmi, J. (2000), *Tertiary Education in the Twenty First Century: Challenges and Opportunities*, World Bank, Washington DC.

Seymour, D. (1992), *On Q: Causing Quality in Higher Education,* Oryx Press, Phoenix.

Sharma, G. D. (2000), *Benchmarks and Performance Indicators for Quality Assurance: The Indian Context,* Paper presented in the Workshop on *Benchmarking and Performance Indicators in Higher Education for Quality Assessment*, Bangalore.

Stella, A. (1999a), A Strategy for Internal Quality Enhancement, *University News*, 37(30), 1-4.

Stella, A. (1999b), Performance Indicators in Quality Assessment: Where do we Draw the Line? *University News*, 37(38), 1-4.

Stella, A. (1999c), Quality Assurance in Higher Education: Long Term Strategy or One-Shot Change? *College News*, Association of

Indian College Principals, December issue, pp.10-12.

Stella, A. (2000a), Ensuring Objectivity in Assessment, *University News*, 38(6), 77-81.

Stella, A. (2000b), In Defence of Autonomy, *University News*, 38(30), 1-5.

Stella, A. (2000c), Moving Forward in the Affiliating System, *University News*, 38(39), 1-4.

Stella, A. (2000d), Best Practices Benchmarking for Quality Assessment, *University News*, 38(45), 1-7.

Stella, A. (2001), Impact of Assessment and Accreditation on Institutions of Higher Education, *University News*, 39(15), 1-4.

Stella, A. and Gnanam, A. (2001a), Institutional Response to Quality Assessment: From Rejection to Appreciation, *QA*, January issue, pp.6-9.

Stella, A. and Gnanam, A. (2001b), Resistance to External Quality Assessment: An Analysis, *University News*, 39(19), 1-4.

Stella, A. and Gnanam, A. (2001c), Institutional Accreditation by NAAC: Scores and Stars, *University News*, 39(36), 50-59.

The University Grants Commission Act 1956 (as modified up to the 20th December 1985) and Rules and Regulations under the Act (1994), University Grants Commission, New Delhi.

Theme paper on NAAC, All India Vice-Chancellor's Conference, Pune, 1994.

Tilak, J. (1994), *Education for Development in Asia*, Sage Publications, New Delhi.

Tilak, J. (1995), Privatisation of Higher Education in India: The Capitation Fee Colleges in Higher Education in India, in *In Search of Quality* (Ed.) Powar, K. B. & Panda, S. K., Association of Indian Universities, New Delhi.

UNESCO (1995), *UNESCO Policy Paper for Change and Development in Higher Education*, UNESCO, Paris.

UNESCO (1996), *Learning: The Treasure Within*, Report of the International Commission on Education for the Twenty First Century (Delors Report), UNESCO, Paris.

UNESCO (1998), *Higher Education in the Twenty-first Century: Vision and Action – Final Report*, UNESCO, Paris.

University Council of Jamaica (1998), *The Accreditation Process*, University Council of Jamaica, Jamaica.

University Grants Commission (UGC) (1987), *Concept Paper for Discussion: Report of the Committee on Accreditation and Assessment*

Council, UGC, New Delhi.

University Grants Commission (UGC) (1990), *Report of the UGC Committee Towards New Educational Management*, UGC, New Delhi.

University Grants Commission (UGC) (1996), *Policy frame and Programs of the UGC: Proposals for the Development of Higher Education in the IX Five Year Plan*, submitted by the Working Group on Higher Education, Planning Commission, UGC, New Delhi.

University Grants Commission (UGC) (1997), *Guidelines for Department/Centre for Adult, Continuing Education, Extension Work and Field Outreach*, UGC, New Delhi.

Vroeijenstijn, A. I. (1995), Government and University: Opponents or Allies in Quality Assurance, *Higher Education Review*, 27(3), 18-36.

Vroeijenstijn, A. I. (1999), *Towards a Quality Hallmark for Higher Education and Towards Mutual Recognition of Quality Assessment Agencies*, Proceedings of the INQAAHE conference at Santiago.

Westerheijden, D. F. and Vught, F. A. van (1994), Towards a General Model of Quality Assessment in Higher Education, *Journal of Higher Education*, 28(3), 355-371.

Woodhouse, D. (1998), Quality Assurance in Higher Education: The Next 25 years, *Quality in Higher Education*, 4(3), 257-73.

Woodhouse, D. (1999), Quality and Quality Assurance, In *Quality and Internationalization in Higher Education*, Imhe Publication.

Woodhouse, D. (2001), *Quality Assurance in Higher Education in the 21st Century*, Address at the Higher Education Quality Committee Inauguration, South Africa.

World Bank (1994), *Higher Education: The Lessons of Experience*, World Bank, Washington DC.

World Bank (2000), *Higher Education in Developing Countries: Peril and Promise*, World Bank, Washington DC.

www.education.nic.in

www.naac-india.com

Yorke, M. (1991), *Performance Indicators: Observations on Their Use in the Assurance of Course Quality*, Council for National Academic Awards Project Report 30, UK.

Yorke, M. (1994), Enhancement-led Higher Education? *Quality Assurance in Education*, 2(3), 6-12.

Young, K. E. *et al.* (Ed.) (1983), *Understanding Accreditation*, Jossey-Bass, San Francisco.

Index